Marlene Pentecost's
NEW COOKBOOK

To God, who gave us life for living.

Published by Elem Pty Ltd,
P.O. Box 130, Glen Waverley, Victoria, Australia, 3150
First published, 1988

Text copyright © Marlene Pentecost, 1988
Photographs copyright © Elem Pty Ltd, 1988

Typeset by Betty Chapman
Printed by Impact Printing, Brunswick, Victoria

Editorial Manager: Celia Pollock
Chief Designer: Sandra Nobes
Photographer: Mike Fisher
Assistant Designer: Lillian Pagonis

ISBN 0 7316 2989 2

The extract on page iv is from *Pritikin People* (Berkley Books, New York, USA, 1986) by
Penelope B. Grenoble, and is reprinted by kind permission of the publisher and Col. Irwin.

Cover Photograph: Mike Fisher

Summer Fruit Tray (page 66)
Chicken in Orange Sauce (page 48) served
with Fruit and Vegetable Salad (page 14)
Cauliflower and Vegetable Soup (page 8)
Orange Juice and Soda (page 85)

Marlene Pentecost's
NEW COOKBOOK

no added salt · no added sugar
no added cholesterol

A bridge to new life

ELEM

FOREWORD

Like many great truths, the dietary message conceived by Nathan Pritikin has become more relevant and obviously true as the years since its first publication pass into decades. So too has the message conveyed by Marlene Pentecost's original book *Cooking for your Life*.

One reflection of the merit of those principles is their increasing acceptance by sceptical medical authorities. Now, the combination of regular exercise with a reduction of dietary fat and simple carbohydrate has enhanced the lives of countless thousands of potential and established victims of degenerative arterial disease.

The problem of dietary modification and substitution in reducing risk factors demands a great deal of our society, oriented as it is towards dangerous food habits.

One of the greatest challenges for all devotees of better dietary habits is to identify ways and means of preparing food and to find enough variety and appeal to ensure continued interest.

It is here that Marlene Pentecost's writings find their mark. She is attuned to both problems and solutions in a tricky area of nutritional knowledge.

Her experience is great. She is a believer. She pioneered the 'new look' at domestic food preparation showing families, singles, novice cooks, the elderly and the young (perhaps the most important group of all) simple ways of improving their dietary habits and thus improving their healthy life expectancy.

This new cookbook from Marlene is a bridge to new life. It extends practical horizons for all who take their diet seriously and safely. Her exciting ideas leave no place for those who would ask 'So what **can** I eat?'. She answers by showing us the abundance of this good earth's riches — in easy recipes for long life.

Professor John Wright, FRACS, FACS
Consultant Cardiac Surgeon

CONTENTS

THOUGHTS ON PRITIKIN LIVING

'...It was a shock to me. I thought, 'Man, Jim Irwin had a heart attack'. Someone who's as physically fit as I am, I have always been a physical fitness nut... I prided myself so much on being strong and healthy.'

'...It's been on my heart for several years to write a book about my experiences with the Pritikin Program. Not only did I regain quality of life, but I can now do things that I thought were finished — like skiing and climbing mountains. And I can do them now with much more zest, much more energy than I ever did, even when I was a young man. I think this should be expressed clearly to encourage those who are facing a similar situation in their own life. And for young people, who could maybe make a change before they are threatened with severe health problems.'

...For independent, strong willed Jim Irwin, to be struck down by a heart attack at 43, in what he thought of as 'the prime of my life,' was quite a blow. 'I always figured,' he concedes, 'that if I could go to the moon, I could do anything, and here I'd had a heart attack. It was a great shock,' he repeats. 'It really hung over me. I realized I was just as weak as others, in fact, I was in worse shape than most.

'...The first summer I went on the Pritikin Program,' he remembers, I was able to climb Pikes Peak (in the Colorado mountains) again. When I got to the top of the mountain, I was jogging — at 14,000 feet. That was something I could never do, even as a young adult.'

'...As astronauts, moving away from the earth, we can see it and realize how precious it is. Logically, we're then obligated to take care of it; we are stewards of the earth. In the Pritikin Program, we... look at our own life... and realize, you know, life is short but here's something I can do... that will extend my life, will add quality to it. And so participating in the Pritikin Program gives us a new perspective on our individual life.'

Colonel James B. Irwin, Astronaut, Apollo 15
(*Two heart attacks and triple by-pass surgery, now fully recovered with the help of the Pritikin Program.*)

With grateful thanks to Jim our 'Brother from the moon' for his permission to reprint these extracts. M.P.

(vi)

INTRODUCTION

In the years since my first book *Cooking for your Life* was published, some wonderful things have happened. Scores of people have been in contact to let me know of the considerable improvement in their health.

Readers of my first book will remember Uncle Harry. He featured in that first preface but now he has recovered from his heart attack and needs no medication. He enjoys walking for about two hours each day. He visits my family on our property two or three times a year and, at 71 years of age, spends his day gardening, building stone walls and pathways, collecting and cutting firewood — all this after his daily walk. I'm sure his stamina would be the envy of many younger men.

If you have had (or are facing) a by-pass operation, regard it as a breathing space to get your life in order. Love your own body — accept the responsibility of caring for it with diet, exercise and a positive attitude.

It doesn't matter how well you fine-tune your car: if you don't put the best fuel into it you won't get the best performance. To get the best out of your body, apply the same theory!

The optimum diet is derived from unprocessed, natural, 'live' foods. To obtain the most vitamins, minerals and enzymes, I suggest fresh vegetables and sprouts (as many as you like) and fruit (eaten raw or juiced). Fresh fruit and vegetable juices should be consumed daily but not as a replacement for whole fruit or vegetables. Go for variety: vegetables can be grated into salads, fill sandwiches, be steamed or cooked in soup. Small amounts of whole grains — cereals, bread, brown rice or wholemeal pasta — should be eaten daily. A small amount of chicken or lean meat is acceptable. For vegetarians, animal protein may be replaced by vegetable protein from legumes (dried beans).

A regular exercise programme is also considered an essential for optimum health and wellbeing. This can be anything from a simple walk to other more strenuous activity, depending on your level of general fitness. A doctor should be consulted prior to entering into any new programme of exercise and particularly if you are in doubt as to the appropriate form your exercise should take. For more information, I recommend you read *The Pritikin Promise*.

This book has been prepared as a continuation from the recipes described in *Cooking for your Life*. The emphasis is on uncomplicated recipes using ingredients that are widely available. I particularly keep in mind those of you who suffer from degenerating disease and those who are trying to avoid health problems in the future. Many of my readers have commented on the particularly legible nature of the print in my first book so I have once again used a large, easily read type to assist those of you whose eyesight is not all it should be!

I hope you will all use this book well, enjoy good health and good living!

Marlene Pentecost
June 1988

Notes

My first book, *Cooking for Your Life* (Reed, Sydney, 1982) contains a similar list of notes to that following. As manufacturers recognise the demand for healthier, low-fat, low-salt, low-sugar foods, more and more 'acceptable' foods become available. That the list below differs from the original is a reflection of changes that have taken place since *Cooking for Your Life* was first published; it will itself change over the years that I hope my *New Cookbook* will remain in print.

BEVERAGES

Drink fruit or vegetable juices straight, or mixed with water, soda water or mineral water. Straight vegetable juices are preferable to fruit juices because of the high natural sugar content in fruit. Try herbal teas or coffee substitutes.

BISCUITS

Try wholemeal matzoh, Ryvita★ (no added salt), whole rye crispbread, Rye 'n Rice★ crispbread and brown rice cakes.

BREAD

Suitable varieties include Pritikin★ wholemeal bread, bread rolls and fruit loaf with cinnamon. Read the list of ingredients on the wrapper if you are unsure about a particular bread, as more and more acceptable breads are coming on to the market.

★ Denotes brand name or registered trade mark.

CAFFEINE

Tea, coffee and cocoa products contain caffeine or theobromine and are to be avoided.

CAKES AND DESSERTS

No commercial products are acceptable. Try limited small serves from recipes in this book. Restrict your consumption of these to keep your triglycerides low.

CANNED PRODUCTS

Use only those packed in water (not brine) or natural juices. DO NOT use diabetic canned fruits as they contain artificial sweeteners.

CHEESE

Use Geska* (Sapsago), low-fat, unsalted cottage cheese or ricotta if less than 2 per cent fat. Check brands for fat content in your State. Recipes using ricotta are **only** acceptable if the ricotta is 2 per cent fat. If not, low-fat unsalted cheese should be substituted. N.B. Geska comes in a shaker pack or in a solid cone shape. The shaker pack has been used for the recipes in this book.

CREAM AND ICE CREAM

No commercial brands are acceptable. Recipes can be found in the Desserts section of this book.

DRIED LEGUMES

These may be eaten daily. They are a good source of protein and fibre; they also make a valuable addition to soup, stews and salads. They are essential to a Regression Diet, replacing animal protein. Soy beans are high in fat and should be restricted to once or twice a week.

EGGS

Use free-range egg whites only. Most health food stores sell free-range eggs.

FATS

All fats, whether saturated or polyunsaturated, are to be avoided. No butter, margarine or fats should be consumed.

* Denotes brand name or registered trade mark.

FLOUR AND GRAINS

Use only wholemeal, stone-ground flour. Cornflour and arrowroot are acceptable for use in thickening.

FRUIT

Eat plenty of fresh fruit in season. Three pieces per day on a Pritikin* Regression Diet; unlimited on a Maintenance Diet.

MEAT

Lean red meat is acceptable on the Pritikin* Diet. The allowed amounts are 100 g per week on the Regression Diet and 100 g per day on the Maintenance Diet. I have chosen not to include any red meat recipes in this book.

MILK AND YOGHURT

Skim milk is used and, unless specified, liquid is used in all recipes. Low-fat yoghurt containing no sugar is used. Jalna* brand is recommended.

PASTA

Use wholemeal spaghetti, lasagna, etc.

POULTRY

Remove skin before cooking. Free-range poultry may be ordered from most health food stores and delicatessens if they are not a regular item.

SALADS

Salads may be eaten as often as you like with as much variety as you can manage. At least one salad daily is essential.

SALT

NONE should be added to any recipes. Check processed food labels to ensure that products are salt-free.

SWEETENERS

No added sugars or artificial sweeteners should be taken. Raisins, dates or fresh fruit may be blended with water or juices to sweeten cakes or desserts.

TAMARI

This is a low sodium variety of soy sauce.

* Denotes brand name or registered trade mark.

TOFU AND SOY PRODUCTS

These may replace the animal protein daily allowance but should not be used more than three times per week.

TOMATO PASTE

Use only Tomato Magic* (pure dehydrated tomato granules) reconstituted with water.

VEGETABLES

Use all varieties raw, juiced, steamed or dry baked. Avocados and olives are the exceptions because of their high fat content. Do not eat or juice rhubarb leaves. Do not combine rhubarb and spinach in the same meal because of the high oxalic content of both.

WINE

Dry white wine or dry sherry may be used in cooking. Cooking eliminates the alcohol content but the flavour is retained.

Measurements

Where possible, measurements are given in cups and spoons. *Spoon* means a rounded spoon, unless otherwise indicated. An Australian *cup* measures 250 mL (8 fl. oz). American spoon and cup measures are different but if all measures in a recipe are by volume, the proportions should still achieve the correct result.

Preparation

The recipes in this book were cooked in a fan-forced oven. A little extra cooking time may be needed if you are using a conventional oven.

A food processor of some kind is a great help in preparing the recipes in this book as many of the fresh ingredients need to be chopped, grated or pureed. I find a Kitchen Whizz* invaluable but any bench-top or wand style processor will suffice. The most important aspect to bear in mind when choosing a brand of food processor is to get the one with the most powerful motor that you can afford.

* Denotes brand name or registered trade mark.

Suggested Shopping List for Beginners

Grains: rolled oats, raw buckwheat, oat bran, millet and linseed (pre-mixed), brown rice, wholemeal pasta, wholemeal self-raising flour, wholemeal matzoh biscuits.

Legumes: dried beans such as kidney and lima beans, lentils (green and red), yellow split peas.

Dried Fruits, Herbs and Spices: Currants, raisins, sultanas, dates, apricots; mixed spice, ginger, nutmeg, cinnamon; powdered chilli, paprika and cummin; granules of garlic and onion; dried leaves of oregano, basil and bay; mixed dried herbs.

Miscellaneous: Carob powder, dry skim milk powder, cornflour, gelatine, herbal teas, coffee substitute, apple cider vinegar, Tomato Magic*, Tamari Sauce* (low sodium soy sauce), Haines Natural Stone-ground Mustard*, Geska* or Sapsago* cheese (shaker pack), pure vanilla essence, unsweetened fruit juice, mineral water, soda water, apple juice concentrate (which resembles clear honey) for sweetening.

In the freezer: fresh fish, skinned chicken breasts, Pritikin* bread, rolls or other acceptable wholemeal breads.

The Tabouli Company* markets some 'no nasties' dehydrated vegetable mixes (including Spicy Vegetable Casserole*) which make an ideal base for vegetable patties, loaves, etc.

There are a few brands of jam available in health food stores that are made only of concentrated fruit, e.g. Whole Earth* brand. In general, the use of jam is limited to keep triglycerides low.

In supermarkets you may find a range of canned fruits, vegetables and fish with reduced, or no salt, sugar, or additives. While I do not advocate a steady diet of these items, they can add a little interest to your diet, or make food preparation a little easier.

At the time of printing, the brand names mentioned were allowable foods. As manufacturers sometimes change or add ingredients without changing the name or packaging style of their products, it is still wise to check all labels carefully.

BREAKFASTS

Muesli

---

500 g rolled oats
250 g unprocessed rice bran
250 g raw buckwheat
175 g millet and linseed
   meal
1 cup sultanas
¼ cup chopped dried apples
¼ cup chopped dried
   apricots

Mix all ingredients together. Store in refrigerator. Serve with skim milk or fresh squeezed orange juice.

If desired, dried fruit may be omitted and fresh fruit sliced on to muesli immediately before serving.

For easier digestion, when having milk with muesli, combine, cover and store in refrigerator overnight. Do not make up ahead of time if having orange juice with muesli. It could be preferable to have fresh fruit for breakfast and muesli later.

Oatmeal

---

1 cup rolled oats
3 cups water
sultanas
nutmeg or cinnamon

Combine oats and water. Stir to avoid catching, and bring to the boil. Reduce heat and cook slowly until mixture becomes thick and creamy — about 15 minutes, stirring occasionally. Add sultanas. Place in serving bowls and lightly dust with nutmeg or cinnamon.

Variations (with or without sultanas)
Stewed apple
Apricot spread (page 83)
Any fresh fruit — sliced banana, chopped or grated apple, blueberries, etc.

Shredded Wheat

2 large shredded wheat
  rolls*
skim milk
1 tablespoon low-fat
  yoghurt
1 tablespoon apricot spread
  (page 83)

Place wheat rolls in bowl. Add milk. Top with yoghurt and apricot spread. If desired, fresh fruit may replace apricot spread.

* At time of printing, Nabisco brand states 100% pure. Read labels carefully.

Per person

Savoury Tomato on Toast

2 slices wholemeal bread
2 dessertspoons tomato
  paste*
1 medium tomato, sliced
1 small onion, finely
  chopped
½ green capsicum, finely
  chopped
Geska cheese
1 tablespoon finely chopped
  parsley

Toast bread, and spread with tomato paste. Place tomato slices on top and cover with onion and capsicum. Sprinkle with Geska cheese. Place under griller for a few minutes. Sprinkle parsley over and serve immediately.

* See cooking notes.

Serves 1

Fruit for Breakfast

Use one cup of seasonal fruits cut into chunks. Serve with a little fresh orange juice squeezed over and/or one dessertspoon of low-fat natural yoghurt spooned over. Top with a sprinkling of Muesli (page 1).

Bubble and Squeak

Mash any quantity of mixed leftover vegetables and form into flat patties. Dry fry slowly in non-stick pan until lightly browned and crisp. Serve on hot wholemeal toast with grilled tomato and a sprinkling of chopped fresh parsley.

Variations
Add a pinch of dried mixed herbs to vegetable mix.
Coat patties with yoghurt topping crumbs (page 82).

Mushrooms on Toast

250 g fresh mushrooms
1 medium onion, cut into rings
¼ cup lemon juice
1 dessertspoon chopped chives
extra chives and slice of lemon for garnish

Place all ingredients in pan and saute for a few minutes only. Do not overcook. Serve on hot wholemeal toast, with a sprinkling of chopped chives and a slice of lemon.

Serves 2

Fruit on Toast

Depending on your choice of fruit, serve it cooked or fresh, warm or cold, on toasted Pritikin* bread.

Suggested combinations:
• Mashed banana with a sprinkling of orange rind.
• Apple with a few sultanas dusted with cinnamon.
• Unsweetened pineapple pieces topped with a little low-fat natural yoghurt and finely chopped mint.

3

Versatile Vegi

2 large tomatoes, coarsely
    chopped
1 medium onion, cut into
    rings
1 cup steamed potato, cut
    into chunks
1 tablespoon finely chopped
    garlic chives
toast for serving

Place all ingredients except chives in a non-stick pan. Cover and cook over medium heat 5-10 minutes, stirring occasionally to prevent sticking. Add chives and serve with hot toast immediately.

Variations
Other leftover steamed vegetables may be included. Other fresh herbs could replace garlic chives. Use as a filling for crepes (page 58) or other stuffed vegetables, e.g. capsicum, eggplant, squash, etc.

Serves 2

Judy's Baked Beans

1 can (410 g) tomatoes
1 cup water
1 cup tomato paste*
1 large clove garlic
1 small onion
¼ teaspoon chilli powder
½ teaspoon oregano
1 packet 'Great Northern'
    beans, cooked

Place all ingredients except beans into blender. Process until smooth. Combine with beans in large saucepan. Cover and simmer about 1 hour.

    For this recipe, the beans must be fully cooked as the acid in tomatoes prevents further cooking.

    Beans may be frozen into serving portions.

N.B. This recipe is best with Great Northern beans, usually obtainable from continental delicatessens. Haricot or any small white beans are acceptable substitutes if you cannot get Great Northern.

* See cooking notes.

Fruit for Breakfast, Oatmeal, Shredded Wheat (pages 1/2)

APPETIZERS

Fruit Cheese Nibbles

1 cup Dried Fruit Medley★
1 cup orange juice
500 g ricotta cheese†
poppy seeds

Place fruit and juice in saucepan and heat gently to plump fruit. When cold, combine with ricotta cheese and mix well. Form into small balls and roll in poppy seeds. Chill and serve. Store in refrigerator.

Serving suggestion
Serve tucked into green lettuce leaves, around Crisp Apple Individual (page 19).

† See cooking notes.
★ Dried Fruit Medley available at supermarket.

Garlic and Bean Paté

1 cup cooked mixed beans
  (legumes)
2 tablespoons lemon juice
1 teaspoon tamari
2 teaspoons fresh chopped
  garlic
½ cup chopped parsley
1 tablespoon water

Combine all ingredients and blend or process until smooth.

Serving suggestion
Serve on bread shapes lightly toasted in warm oven, as a dip, or with a small salad as an entree.

N.B. The garlic is very strong and, if desired, the quantity could be halved.

Makes 1 cup

Oriental Soup (page 10)
Sweet Potato and Broccoli Soup (page 8)
Cauliflower and Vegetable Soup (page 8)

Potato Canapés

**Tiny new potatoes,
  scrubbed and steamed
Sour Cream Dressing
  (page 80)**

Cut potatoes in half and spoon over a little Sour Cream Dressing. Top Sour Cream Dressing with any of the following:
- Chopped fresh herbs, e.g. chives, coriander
- basil
- horseradish
- Geska cheese
- celery
- garlic
- beansprouts
- grated carrot
- broccoli florets (tiny)

Variation
- Use cherry tomatoes cut in half and topped as above.
- Use small button mushrooms, wiped clean and with stalks removed. Fill with Sour Cream Dressing and top with any of the suggestions above.

Chick Pea Nibbles

225 g chick peas

Cover with water and bring to the boil. Remove saucepan from heat and let it stand for 2 hours or longer. Drain water from pan and cover chick peas generously with fresh cold water. Bring to the boil and cook about 1 hour, until tender. Drain water off and stir over medium heat until peas dry out and brown. Do not burn. Peas may be eaten as a nibble to replace peanuts, etc. Store in airtight jar.

N.B. Do not overcook peas or they will go soft and mushy. If this happens, peas may be dried out by placing in a just warm oven, on a baking tray, for about 15 minutes.

SOUPS

Chicken Stock

1 chicken (free range),
  whole or pieces
1 large onion
2 medium carrots
2 stalks celery, with tops
1 bouquet garni

Remove skin and visible fat from chicken. Trim, clean and chop vegetables. Place all ingredients in a large saucepan and cover with cold water. Bring to boil and simmer 2 hours. Strain and pour liquid into bowl. Refrigerate until stock is set and fat is solidified on surface. Remove fat. Reheat until stock is of a pouring consistency. Pour into ice cube containers and freeze. Remove stock cubes from containers and store in freezer bags in freezer. Use as a base for sauces, casseroles and soup.

Vegetable Stock

potatoes (with peel if
  scrubbed clean)
carrots
onions
celery (including tops)
swede
parsnip
tomatoes
bouquet garni

Trim, clean and chop vegetables. Place in saucepan and cover with cold water. Bring to boil and simmer 1 hour. Remove from heat and allow to cool. Pour into ice cube containers and freeze. Remove stock cubes from containers and store in freezer bags in freezer. Use as a base for sauces and soups.

Celery and Onion Soup

2 medium onions, cut into
   rings
2 sticks celery, chopped
2 cups chicken stock
2½ cups skim milk
2 tablespoons cornflour
2 slices wholemeal bread
Geska cheese

Place onions, celery, chicken stock and 2 cups of the milk in a saucepan. Bring to the boil and simmer 30 minutes. Remove saucepan from heat and quickly stir in cornflour mixed with remaining ½ cup of milk. Return to low heat and simmer further 5 minutes. At this time, place bread under griller and toast on one side. Sprinkle cheese on untoasted side and grill until cheese melts. Cut cheese toast into small squares and float on top of soup when serving.

Serves 4

Cauliflower and Vegetable Soup

4 cups chicken stock
¼ large cauliflower
1 medium potato
1 medium carrot
1 stick celery
1 medium onion
2 tablespoons dry sherry

Place stock in large saucepan. Roughly chop vegetables. Add vegetables to stock and bring to boil. Simmer 30 minutes, or longer if desired. Process soup in blender or electric mixer until smooth. Return to saucepan. Add sherry and reheat.

Serving suggestion
Top with chopped fresh coriander or parsley.

Serves 4

Sweet Potato and Broccoli Soup

1.5 kg red sweet potato
1 large head broccoli
1 large onion
chicken stock (about 1.5 L)

Peel and chop sweet potato into chunks. Chop broccoli and onion into chunks. Place vegetables in 3-litre saucepan and cover them with chicken stock. Cover saucepan and bring to the boil. Reduce heat and

parsley, finely chopped, for garnish

simmer for 1 hour. Transfer soup from saucepan to blender and process till smooth. Reheat and serve with a sprinkling of parsley.

N.B. If broccoli stalks are 'woody', discard.

Serves 4

Tomato Soup

---

1 can (410 g) tomatoes
1 tablespoon tomato granules★
1 small onion
1 stick celery
1 cup skim milk
½ cup cooked brown rice (optional)
chopped fresh herbs

Place tomatoes with liquid, tomato granules, onion and celery in blender. Process to liquefy. Pour into saucepan and bring to boil. Reduce heat and simmer. Add milk and rice. Simmer 15 minutes, stirring occassionally. Serve with chopped fresh parsley, chives, or coriander and toast.

If a richer flavour is desired, add 1 garlic clove chopped and 1 teaspoon each of dried basil and oregano.

If a thicker soup is required, a little cornflour mixed with water could be added while stirring.

★ See cooking notes.

Serves 4

Garden Carrot Soup

---

6 cups chicken stock
1.5 kg carrots
2 medium new potatoes
2 sticks celery
1 medium onion
1 garlic clove
1 cup skim milk
6 shallots
½ cup chopped parsley
½ cup chopped mint

Place stock in large saucepan. Scrub and chop carrots and potatoes. Peel and chop other vegetables. Add celery, onion and garlic to stock. Cover, bring to the boil, then simmer 30 minutes or longer if desired. Pour ⅔ of the stock from the saucepan into the blender and process it until smooth. Return the processed stock to saucepan. Heat through. Immediately before serving, add milk, shallots, parsley and mint.

Serves 6

Pumpkin Soup

6 cups chicken stock
1.25 kg pumpkin
1 large stick celery
3 medium carrots
1 large onion
½ cup skim milk
light sprinkling of nutmeg
chopped fresh coriander or
    parsley
3 tablespoons Sour Cream
    Dressing (optional)
    (page 80)

Place stock in large saucepan. Peel, trim or scrub vegetables and cut into large chunks. Place vegetables in saucepan, cover and bring to boil. Lower heat and simmer 1½ hours. Transfer vegetables from saucepan to blender and puree with a little stock. Return vegetables to saucepan, adding milk and nutmeg. Reheat and serve with a sprinkling of coriander or parsley. (Coriander gives the soup a little bite.) If you have some, place a teaspoon of Sour Cream Dressing on top of each serve.

N.B. The pumpkin should be bright yellow in colour. New pumpkin is pale and does not have a strong enough flavour for this soup.

Serves 6

Oriental Soup

6 cups chicken stock
½ cup dry sherry
1 tablespoon tamari
1 medium onion, chopped
1 medium carrot, roughly
    grated
1 medium zucchini, roughly
    grated
1 portion rice vermicelli*
3 shallots chopped
chopped garlic and grated
    fresh ginger (optional)

Place all ingredients except vermicelli and shallots in saucepan. Simmer for 30 minutes, then add vermicelli and cook a further 5 minutes. Sprinkle shallots on top when serving.

* Rice vermicelli is purchased from Chinese grocery stores and some delicatessens, and is packaged in layers of four. One portion equals one layer. More or less may be used as desired.

Serves 6

SALADS

Coleslaw

¼ medium savoy (green)
   cabbage
2 medium carrots
1 medium onion
2 medium zucchini
2 tablespoons Sour Cream
   Dressing (page 80)

Finely shred or grate vegetables (in a food processor is best).

   Place vegetables in bowl and add Sour Cream Dressing. Toss to mix, and serve.

Serves 4

Potato Salad

---

750 g new potatoes
1 medium onion, chopped
1 cup chopped celery
½ cup chopped fresh mint
2 tablespoons Sour Cream
   Dressing (page 80)

Leaving skin on, wash and scrub potatoes. Chop into chunks and steam about 10 minutes, until cooked but not soft. While still hot, add onion, celery and mint. Toss to mix, adding Sour Cream Dressing immediately before serving.

Serving suggestion
Serve as an entree, on lettuce leaves, or filling whole tomatoes or capsicums.

Variation
Use tiny whole potatoes. The cooking time would be the same. Decorate with tiny cherry tomatoes, halved.

N.B. Do not eat potato sprouts or potatoes with a green appearance.

11

Beetroot and Carrot Salad

2 medium beetroot
2 medium carrots
Lemon and Garlic Dressing
  (page 81)
Lemon slices

Trim, peel and roughly grate beetroot. Trim, scrub and roughly grate carrots. Combine and lightly mix. Sprinkle dressing over and serve with lemon slices.

N.B. Peel beetroot to avoid 'earthy' taste. It is not necessary to peel carrots.

Serves 4

Carrot and Orange Salad

2 medium carrots
1 medium red apple
1 orange (juice and finely
  grated rind)
½ cup sultanas
lettuce leaves
mint sprigs

Scrub and roughly grate carrots. Slice unpeeled apple into fine slivers. Pour orange juice over apple to avoid discolouration. Combine carrots and apple with juice, orange rind and sultanas. Arrange in a dish lined with lettuce leaves, and place mint sprigs on top.

Serves 4

Orange Salad

2 medium sweet oranges,
  thinly sliced
1 medium onion, sliced into
  rings
2 teaspoons finely chopped
  mint

Interleave and overlap orange and onion slices in circles. Sprinkle mint over and serve.

Serves 2-4

Crunchy Vegetarian Salad

1 medium carrot
1 medium zucchini
¼ small savoy (green) cabbage
½ cup cauliflower florets
½ cup broccoli florets
½ cup finely chopped celery
lettuce leaves, torn
endive leaves, torn
alfalfa sprouts
herb vinegar

Roughly grate carrot, zucchini and cabbage. Place in bowl and add other vegetables and sprouts, tossing well. Just before serving, add a sprinkling of vinegar and toss.

Serves 4-6

Salad Greens with a Bite

1 small lettuce
1 small bunch endive
1 small bunch watercress
1 small onion, cut into rings
1 cup alfalfa sprouts

Wash and tear lettuce and endive leaves. Wash watercress and break into sprigs. Place in bowl, adding onion rings and sprouts. Toss lightly to mix.

Serving suggestion
Accompany with Lemon and Garlic Dressing (page 81).

Serves 4

Red Cabbage Salad

½ small head red cabbage, finely shredded
2 stalks celery, finely chopped
1 small onion, finely chopped
1 cup alfalfa sprouts

Combine, toss and serve with herb vinegar or Sour Cream Dressing (page 80).

Serves 4

13

Fruit and Vegetable Salad

1 can (440 g) unsweetened
   pineapple pieces
1 red apple, unpeeled,
   roughly chopped
1 medium carrot, cut in
   julienne strips
1 medium green capsicum,
   finely sliced and chopped
100 g fresh mung
   beansprouts, rinsed in
   cold water*
small head endive leaves
¼ cup chopped fresh
   coriander

Drain pineapple. Use a little of the juice to pour over apple (to avoid discolouration) and toss. Combine all ingredients, tossing lightly. Place in serving dish and serve immediately.

* Commercially grown, Chinese-style.

Serves 4

Pawpaw Chicken Salad Plate

1 cup cooked chicken,
   chopped or minced
½ cup Sour Cream Dressing
   (page 80)
¼ cup chopped chives
1 small, ripe pawpaw

Combine chicken with Sour Cream Dressing and chives. Cut pawpaw in half and remove seeds. Cut a small piece from underneath, to allow fruit to sit without toppling. Fill cavity with chicken mixture and place in centre of plate.

The salad accompaniment is your choice. My suggestion is as follows:

On one quarter of the plate place a few strawberries, pineapple pieces and kiwifruit slices. Next a few fresh, crisp snow peas, followed by some torn lettuce or endive topped with grated zucchini and carrot, and a finely sliced mushroom. Lastly, cut a piece of Pritikin bread into triangles and place, overlapping, on a plate. Garnish with parsley sprigs and alfalfa sprouts.

Variation
Turkey or salmon may replace chicken. Pawpaw may be replaced by scooped out pineapple halves. Pineapple chunks may be included in filling.

N.B. If small pawpaws are unavailable, use one quarter of a large fruit per person.

Tangy Green Bean Salad

500 g stringless fresh green beans
½ cup Lemon and Garlic Dressing (page 81)
finely grated rind of 1 lemon

Trim ends and wash beans. Drop whole beans into boiling water and cook 3 or 4 minutes, until beans are cooked but still crisp. Drain and immediately rinse with cold water 3 times, to stop beans cooking in their own heat and to ensure they retain their bright green colour. Arrange in long, narrow salad dish and pour dressing over, followed by a sprinkling of lemon rind.

Serves 2-4

Mushroom and Herb Salad

2 cups sliced small mushrooms
½ cup 'mint and marjoram' vinegar
lettuce leaves
1 tablespoon Sour Cream Dressing (page 80)
1 tablespoon finely chopped fresh mint

Marinate mushrooms in vinegar for 1 hour or longer. Arrange lettuce leaves in serving dish. Place mushrooms on lettuce, spoon Sour Cream Dressing over and sprinkle with mint.

Variation
Other herb vinegars may replace 'mint and marjoram'. The mint should then be replaced by a fresh herb to complement the vinegar.

Serves 4

Merry-go-round Salad

1 medium green skin
  cucumber, unpeeled and
  finely sliced
2 medium tomatoes, finely
  sliced
1 medium onion, finely cut
  into rings
Sour Cream and Garlic
  Dressing (page 81)
½ cup chopped chives

On a circular plate, arrange the ingredients in the order listed, in an overlapping circular pattern, from the outside in. Place a spoonful of dressing in the centre, and sprinkle the chives over all.

Serves 2

Mushroom and Beansprout Salad

500 g cultured mushrooms,
  sliced
250 g Chinese mung
  beansprouts*
1 small lettuce, torn

Combine mushrooms, beansprouts and lettuce. Toss lightly to mix.

Serving suggestions
Accompany with 1 cup Yoghurt Topping Crumbs (page 82) and 1 cup Sour Cream Dressing (page 80). For individual serves, sprinkle Topping Crumbs over and spoon a little Sour Cream Dressing into the centre.

★ Commercially grown, Chinese-style.

Serves 4

Pasta Salad with Tomato Sauce

250 g cooked wholemeal
  spaghetti pasta (cold)
½ cup cooked corn niblets
½ cup finely chopped celery

If necessary, rinse pasta to separate. Chop spaghetti into small pieces. Combine all ingredients except sauce. Toss to mix.

16

½ cup finely sliced button
mushrooms
½ red capsicum, finely
chopped
¼ cup finely chopped
coriander
2 cups Basic Tomato Sauce
(page 83)

Serving suggestion
Serve as an entree or in a serving dish for a buffet
table. Accompany with a jug of Basic Tomato Sauce.

Serves 4

Carrot, Sprout and Mushroom Salad

1 small lettuce, torn
1 cup alfalfa sprouts
1 cup sliced button
mushrooms
1 stick celery, finely
chopped
½ cup chopped raisins
1 small carrot, grated
½ cup coarsely chopped
coriander

Place all in serving dish. Toss to mix.

Variation
Coriander could be replaced with watercress. Lettuce
could be replaced with endive.

Serving suggestion
Serve with any variation of Sour Cream Dressing
(page 80).

Serves 4

Brown Rice and Apple Salad

2 cups Cooked Apple Rice
(page 44)
¼ teaspoon powdered
ginger
1 cup chopped celery
½ cup coarsely chopped
raisins
1 medium red apple

Place all ingredients except apple in bowl, and lightly
mix.
    Chop and add apple immediately before serving to
avoid discolouration.

Variation
Add 1 cup drained unsweetened pineapple pieces.

Serves 4

Pasta Salad with Sour Cream Dressing

250 g cooked wholemeal
  spaghetti (cold)
¼ cup finely chopped
  shallots
¼ cup finely chopped chives
¾ cup Sour Cream Dressing
  (page 80)
tiny cherry tomatoes,
  halved
lettuce leaves

Combine pasta, shallots and chives. Toss to mix. Place on individual flat plates, then place a dessertspoon of Sour Cream Dressing on top of each. To one side, arrange tomatoes nestling in lettuce leaves. Sour Cream Dressing and pasta should be tossed to combine at time of eating.

Serving suggestion
Serve as an entree or on a large serving platter for a buffet table. Accompany with Sour Cream Dressing.

Serves 4

Fresh Green Herb Salad

1 small lettuce
1 small bunch endive
1 small apple cucumber,
  peeled and finely chopped
½ green capsicum, seeded
  and finely sliced
2 tablespoons chopped
  chives
2 tablespoons chopped mint
1 tablespoon lemon thyme,
  leaves only, discard stalks
herb vinegar

Tear lettuce and endive into pieces. Place in bowl and add all ingredients except vinegar. Toss well. Add a sprinkling of herb vinegar when serving.

Variation
Other dressings in this book may replace vinegar.

Serves 4

18

Crisp Apple Individual

endive and celery leaves
1 red apple unpeeled
orange juice
small bunch grapes
1 dessertspoon yoghurt or
   ricotta cheese

Place endive and celery leaves on plate. Core and slice apple into quarters. Pour orange juice over apple. Place apple on plate, standing the pieces up or lying them in a circle. Spoon yoghurt or ricotta cheese in centre, positioning grapes on top.

If using red apple, use green grapes. If using green apple, use black grapes.

Variations
Frozen grapes are delicious. Select small bunches and place uncovered in freezer for 24 hours. Do not remove until the moment of serving, as grapes will blush and should be eaten immediately.

N.B. Lettuce may replace endive and celery.

Serving suggestion
Great as an entree, snack or dessert. Try Fruit Cheese Nibbles (page 5) as an accompaniment.

Per person

Bean Salad

3 cups cooked mixed beans
1 medium onion, finely
   chopped
1 medium capsicum, finely
   chopped
1 tablespoon lemon juice
2 tablespoons chopped mint
2 tablespoons apple cider
   vinegar

Combine and mix ingredients at least 1 hour before serving.

Variation
Herb flavoured vinegars, e.g. mint and marjoram, lemon and garlic, etc. may replace apple cider vinegar and lemon juice.

Serves 4-6

VEGETABLES

Steamed Vegetables

Method for any vegetables

Place steaming basket in saucepan. Add enough water to fill up to the base of the basket. Vegetables may be mixed, and cooked together if desired. Be careful to cut those vegetables requiring more cooking into smaller pieces so they will be cooked at the same time as the other vegetables. When steaming commences, lower heat but ensure water is still boiling underneath. Start timing. Vegetables should take about 10-15 minutes, they should be bright in colour if they are not overcooked.

Some suitable mixed vegetable combinations:
Potato and pumpkin, diced, and cauliflower and broccoli, cut small, will cook in the same time as peas and beans. Vegetables may be cooked separately, adjusting the time to suit the size of the vegetables.

Serving suggestion
Accompany with a jug of any of the sauces (see index) piping hot, or sprinkle with fresh herbs, chopped raw onion or lemon juice.

N.B. When steaming commences, do not lift lid until cooking is completed. Be careful to have enough water in saucepan so it won't boil dry.

Fresh Asparagus

---

1 bundle asparagus
Geska cheese

Trim fibrous ends off asparagus stalks. Place asparagus flat in steamer. Cover and cook for 10 minutes. Place on warm serving dish and sprinkle with Geska cheese. Serve immediately.

Variation
To serve hot, replace Geska with a little White Sauce with lemon or parsley (page 79).
To serve cold, replace geska with Lemon and Garlic Dressing (page 81).

Snow Peas

Trim ends of peas and remove side string. Place in steaming basket over boiling water. Cover and cook for 2 minutes only. Peas should be crunchy and bright green.

To serve peas cold with salad, wash well under cold water. Trim ends and remove side string. Place in cold water for at least 5 minutes, to refresh before serving.

Minted Spinach

½ cup chopped mint
¼ cup apple cider vinegar
1 medium bunch spinach

Pour boiling water over mint until it is just covered, and allow to stand 5 minutes to draw flavour from the mint. Add vinegar, stir and set aside.

Wash and finely chop spinach. Steam about 5 minutes, until just cooked.

Stir sauce lightly through hot spinach and serve immediately.

Bean and Spinach Loaf (page 37)
Vegetarian Chilli Beans (page 40)
Chicken in Orange Sauce (page 48)

Chilled Beetroot

1 bunch beetroot
apple cider vinegar

Trim stalks of beetroot, leaving about 5 centimetres (2 inches). Place beetroot in a steamer saucepan. Cover and steam — about 30 minutes for small beetroot, 60 minutes for large. Insert a knife to determine if tender and cooked. Discard skin and slice. Pour vinegar over each layer of beetroot, making sure final layer is covered with vinegar. Cover basin and refrigerate.

Ginger Cabbage

fresh savoy (green) cabbage, shredded
2 teaspoons grated ginger
¾ cup water

Place cabbage in pan, adding ginger mixed with water. Stir to mix. Cover and steam about 4 minutes. Serve immediately.

Variation
Grated apple and/or grated zucchini and carrot may be added to cabbage.

Serving suggestion
Serve with Golden Chicken with Apricot (page 47).

Beetroot with Garlic

4 medium size beetroot
4 cloves garlic, chopped
juice of 2 lemons

Trim beetroot stalks, leaving about 5 centimetres (2 inches). Steam beetroot about 45 minutes. Mix garlic with lemon juice to make a dressing. Discard skin from beetroot while hot. Chop into large chunks and pour dressing over. Serve hot as an entree or an extra vegetable, or cold as a salad dish.

N.B. Beetroot may be baked whole in the oven at 200°C (400°F) for about 1 hour, depending on size. Do not prick skin. Serve as above.

Serves 4

Ginger Spinach

½ cup chicken stock
1 dessertspoon tamari
1 teaspoon grated ginger
1 clove garlic, chopped
1 teaspoon lemon juice
1 medium bunch spinach

Place stock, tamari, ginger, garlic and lemon juice in saucepan. Gently heat and keep hot.

Sprinkle a little water in a non-stick pan. Wash and finely chop spinach. Place in pan. Cover and cook for 5 minutes on a moderate heat, shaking the pan to prevent scorching.

Stir sauce into spinach and serve immediately.

Serves 4

Crunchy Garlic Garden Vegetables

4 cups lightly steamed
    mixed vegetables (do not
    overcook) e.g. peas, green
    beans, celery, carrots,
    zucchini
2 cups Garlic Crumbed
    Yoghurt Toast Topping
    (page 82)

Place hot vegetables on individual entree dishes and sprinkle crumbed topping over. Serve immediately.

Serving suggestion
Use as an entree, to be followed by spaghetti, or as a luncheon dish, served with green salad.

Variation
Top vegetables with other Yoghurt Toast Toppings (page 82).

Serves 4

Chinese Vegetables

1 cup carrots, sliced
1 cup broccoli florets
1 cup cauliflower florets
1 large onion, cut in half
   across and quarters
   lengthways
1 cup zucchini, thickly
   sliced
2 cloves garlic, chopped
1 teaspon grated root ginger
½ cup water
4 teaspoons tamari
1 tablespoon dry sherry
1 cup chicken stock
1 cup button mushrooms,
   roughly chopped
200 g mung beansprouts
   (commercially grown)
200 g snow peas
4 teaspoons cornflour mixed
   with 2 tablespoons
   cold water
½ cup chopped shallots

Put carrots, broccoli and cauliflower in a saucepan. Cover and boil rapidly for 3 minutes. Drain immediately and rinse three times with cold water to stop cooking and to retain colour.

In wok or large frying pan, place onion, zucchini, garlic, ginger and about ½ cup water. Stir cook for 2 or 3 minutes. Mix tamari and sherry with stock and pour into pan. Add carrots, broccoli, cauliflower, mushrooms, sprouts and snow peas.

Cover and cook a further 4 minutes. Thicken with cornflour mix. Add shallots and serve immediately with steamed brown rice and/or Garlic Schnapper (page 53).

Variation
Include bite-size pieces of fish when adding second batch of vegetables to wok.

Serves 4

Dry Baked Vegetables

potatoes
sweet potatoes
pumpkin
whole brown onions
choko
whole zucchini

Steam prepared vegetables until cooked, then place on non-stick tray in moderate to hot oven. Cook until vegetables dry out, becoming crisp and brown — about 30 minutes, depending on how hot the oven is. Vegetables will shrink a little, but only the water content is lost, not the goodness.

Hot Herby Greens

3 cups shredded savoy
  (green) cabbage
1 large zucchini, grated
2 stalks celery, chopped
  finely
½ cup chopped fresh herbs
  (basil, chives or
  coriander)

Place cabbage, zucchini and celery in frying pan with a little water to stop them sticking. Cover and cook for 3 or 4 minutes until *just* cooked, preferably still a little crunchy. Quicky stir in herbs and serve immediately.

Serving suggestion
Use as an accompaniment to Potato Chips (page 28) and Salmon and Vegi Loaf (page 56).

Variation
Add grated carrot, onion, red cabbage, capsicum. Serve as an entree, sprinkled with geska cheese or Yoghurt Toast Topping Crumbs (page 82).

Garden Peas

Fresh pods should be full, firm and bright green. Remove peas from pod, and steam about 5 minutes.

Variation
Chopped mint may be added to peas when steaming. When serving, a little Mint Sauce (page 81) may be stirred through.

Sugar Peas

Trim ends of peas only. Do not remove from pods, and steam as above.

25

Sweet Potato and Apple Casserole

1 medium to large *red* sweet
   potato
2 large apples
¾ cup unsweetened apple
   juice

Peel potatoes and apples. Slice thinly. Place in a casserole dish in alternate layers, starting with apples and finishing with potato. Pour juice over. Cover and bake in moderate oven, 200°C (400°F), about 45 minutes. Remove lid and bake further 15 minutes. Potatoes should be reasonably soft when cooked.

Serving suggestion
This recipe is equally delicious served hot wth a main meal or cold with a salad. It is a good party dish in a larger quantity.

Apple Jacket Potatoes

4 large new potatoes
2 large apples, cooked
1 cup chopped celery
low-fat yoghurt

Scrub clean and pierce potatoes. Cook in skins in moderate to hot oven 200°C (425°F) until tender —about 1 hour. Slice tops off, leaving a cavity in each potato. Combine apple and celery and fill potatoes. Replace tops and brush generously with yoghurt. Place on non-stick tray and cook a further 10-15 minutes. Tops should be crisp.

Variation
Cut deep grooves lengthways in each cooked potato. Fill grooves and brush top with a mixture of low-fat yoghurt and chopped chives. Sprinkle Geska cheese over and reheat 10-15 minutes.

Serving suggestion
Serve as an entree or with Chicken Parcels (page 48) and Steamed Green Vegetables (page 20).

Serves 4

26

Beansprouts Oriental

1 small onion, finely
  chopped
1 teaspoon finely grated
  ginger
1 clove garlic, finely
  chopped
4 tablespoons water
2 tablespoons dry sherry
2 tablespoons tamari
1 teaspoon cornflour
2 cups Chinese mung
  beansprouts
  (commercially grown)

Place onion, ginger and garlic in a non-stick pan with 2 tablespoons of the water. Over moderate heat, stir for 1 minute. Combine sherry, tamari, remaining water and cornflour. Add to pan and stir to mix. Add beansprouts and toss to mix. Cook 1 or 2 minutes to heat beansprouts, and serve immediately.

Serving suggestion
Serve with Chicken Parcels (page 48).

Variation
If sauce is required, add 1 cup of chicken stock to sherry, tamari and water. Increase thickening to 1 dessertspoon of cornflour to 2 tablespoons of water.

Serves 4

Seasoned Potato Patties

3 medium potatoes
1 cup corn niblets (fresh or
  frozen)
1 medium apple, grated
½ cup chopped shallots
⅓ cup chopped chives
1 egg white
skim milk
fine wholemeal
  breadcrumbs

Steam and mash potatoes. Add corn, apple, shallots, and chives to hot potato. Mix egg white with a little skim milk and add to mix. Form into patties and cover with breadcrumbs. Place on a non-stick tray and bake at 200°C (400°F) for 15-20 minutes or until golden.

Serving suggestion
Serve with Pepita Bean and Vegetable Delight (page 36).

Variation
Coat patties in Geska Cheese Yoghurt Toast Crumbs (page 82). This will give a crunchy cheese flavour.

Serves 4

Potato Chips

any quantity of large old potatoes

Peel and wash potatoes. Slice into 3 or 4 big slices about 1 cm (½ inch) thick. Steam until just cooked.

Carefully remove slices from steamer and place on a large non-stick tray. Cut into chips, separating as you cut. Put tray into oven and bake. Flip chips over once or twice until crisp and brown. Serve immediately.

Cooking times
Hot oven, about 15 minutes
Moderate oven, about 20 minutes
Slow oven, about 30 minutes.

N.B. Oven temperature does not matter, as long as it is kept constant during cooking.

Bean and Lentil Burger

2 cups cooked beans (legumes)
1 cup cooked brown lentils
1 egg white
1 small onion, finely chopped
1 cup soft breadcrumbs
1 level teaspoon dried sage
½ level teaspoon dried thyme
small amount of stock or water for moistening
fine breadcrumbs for crumbing

Place beans, lentils and egg white into a food processor and process until smooth. Add onion, breadcrumbs and herbs, processing until smooth. If mixture is too dry, add a little stock or water.

Form flat patties and cover with fine breadcrumbs. Cook in non-stick pan, over moderate to low heat — about 10 minutes — flipping over after 5 minutes.

Serving suggestion
Serve with a salad filling in a toasted wholemeal bun.

Serves 4

Jacket Baked Potatoes

4 medium potatoes

(Fillings are listed below basic recipe)

Wash and scrub potatoes well. Pat dry. Pierce several times with fork. Place in hot oven 220°C (425°F) and bake for 1 hour. For a softer skin, wrap potatoes in foil and bake 45 minutes. Cut an angled slice from the top of each potato. Scoop out the potato, mix with chosen filling and replace into skin. Replace top and serve immediately.

Fillings for potato as an extra vegetable:
Sour Cream and Chives (page 80).
Horseradish Cream (page 80).
Herb and Breadcrumb Seasoning (page 74).

Fillings for potato as a main vegetable:
(Spoon the following hot fillings into and over potato.)
Vegetarian Chilli Beans (page 40).
Stewed Tomato and Onion (page 34).
Reheated leftovers, e.g. Vegetarian Goulash (page 38).

Serving suggestion
Can be served as a main vegetable. Also serve with other vegetables, or with salad, as an entree or luncheon dish.

N.B. If using for a main vegetable, larger potatoes are required. Cooking time may need to be increased slightly.

Serves 4

Flat Potato Cakes

1 large potato
1 small onion, finely
  chopped
1 egg white

Peel potato, cut into quarters and steam until just cooked (not soft). Allow to cool, then roughly grate and combine with onion and egg white. Lightly toss. Heat a non-stick pan and place a thin layer of mixture in, not quite covering the bottom. Separate into pikelet-size cakes. Cook over moderate to slow heat about 10 minutes, until crisp and brown. When cooked, place uncovered in warm to moderate oven to keep hot while remainder cooks. Serve while hot.

Variation
Substitute pumpkin for potato.
1 tablespoon fresh chopped herbs may be added.

Serving suggestion
Can be served with Chicken Parcels with Minted Spinach (page 48) and grilled tomatoes.

Serves 4

Potato and Herb Layer

3 medium new potatoes
1 large onion
1 cup chopped, fresh herbs
  (one kind, or mixed)
1 cup non-fat yoghurt

Use a non-stick oven dish. Peel, wash and thinly slice potatoes and onion, separating onion rings. Arrange in graduating circles, from the outside, in the following order: First, the potatoes. Then brush with yoghurt. Follow with the onion rings, then sprinkle with the fresh herbs. Continue in this manner, finishing with potatoes, and brush the top with yoghurt.
  Cover and bake 45 minutes at 200°C (400°F). Uncover and bake an extra 15 minutes or longer if necessary. Garnish with a sprinkling of fresh herbs and serve immediately.

Serving suggestion
Serve with Saucy Jewfish Cutlets (page 53), steamed carrots, and peas.

Variation
Replace yoghurt with Basic Tomato Sauce (page 83). Cover and bake for 45 minutes. Serve as an entree with a small green salad — garnish with chopped parsley.

Serves 4

Ratatouille and Potato Bake

Topping
750 g potatoes
2 tablespoons skim milk
1 medium onion, chopped
½ cup chopped chives
Geska cheese (optional)

Prepare topping ready for use before cooking the filling.

Dice potatoes and steam until cooked, about 10 minutes. While hot, add milk, onion and chives. Mash together.

Filling
1 large onion, sliced into rings
3 medium zucchini, sliced
2 medium tomatoes, cut into chunks
2 cups mushrooms, roughly chopped
1 cup sprouted mung beans
1 cup corn niblets
½ teaspoon dried basil
½ teaspoon dried oregano

Place all filling ingredients in a non-stick pan. Cover and cook about 5 minutes over a medium heat, shaking the pan to prevent catching. Pour into an ovenproof dish and cover with topping. Sprinkle with Geska cheese and bake 30 minutes in a moderate oven 200°C (400°F).

Variation
Replace corn with cooked beans (legumes).

Serves 6

Filled Butternut Pumpkin

1 small butternut pumpkin
1 cup Herb and
   Breadcrumb Seasoning
   (page 74)

Thoroughly scrub pumpkin clean. Cut in half length-ways and steam until cooked. (Cooking time will depend on size of pumpkin.) Remove seeds and fill cavity with seasoning. Place in a moderate oven 200°C (400°F) about 15 minutes, to reheat pumpkin and cook seasoning.

Serving suggestion
Serve with Dry Baked Potatoes (page 24), steamed cauliflower and steamed green beans.

Variation
Fill with tomato, onion and breadcrumbs or cooked rice, or any suitable leftovers from previous day, e.g. Tuna (page 56).

Serves 2

Zucchini with Seasoning

2 large tomatoes, sliced
1 medium onion, cut into
   rings
2 large zucchini, sliced
1 quantity Herb and Breadcrumb Seasoning
   (page 74)

In an oven dish, place layers of tomatoes, onion and zucchini. Sprinkle seasoning over, and finish with a layer of tomatoes. Bake uncovered 45 minutes at 200°C (400°F).

Serving suggestion
Serve with Minted Spinach Chicken Parcels (page 48) and steamed green beans.

Serves 4

Crunchy Vegetarian Pie

1 medium potato
1 medium red sweet potato
1 medium carrot
1 medium zucchini
1 small onion
½ cup chopped shallots
½ cup chopped fresh herbs
 (coriander or chives)
1 cup breadcrumbs
1 egg white
Geska Cheese Yoghurt
 Toast Topping (page 82)

Grate potatoes, carrot, zucchini and onion. Add shallots, herbs, breadcrumbs and egg white. Mix well. Press into a non-stick ovenproof dish. Bake 20 minutes in moderate oven 200°C (400°F). Then top with Geska Cheese Yoghurt Toast Topping (page 82) and bake a further 15 minutes, or until topping is golden and crunchy.

Serving suggestion
Serve hot with Steamed Cauliflower in White Parsley Sauce (page 79) and Steamed Snow Peas (page 21). Serve Basic Tomato Sauce (page 83) as an accompaniment. Serve cold with salad.

Serves 4

Garlic Spinach with Rice

1 small bunch spinach
2 cups cooked rice
2 cloves garlic, finely
 chopped
½ cup fresh chopped
 coriander
Geska cheese

Wash and finely chop spinach. Place, with a little water, in a non-stick pan. Add garlic and rice. Cover and steam for 5 minutes, stirring occasionally to avoid sticking. Uncover. Stir in coriander. Serve immediately, sprinkling a little Geska cheese on top.

Serving suggestion
Serve as an entree, or with Toasted Asparagus Roll Ups (page 76) and Yoghurt Coated Jacket Potatoes (page 26).

Variation
Use cabbage instead of spinach and any other fresh or dried herbs to replace coriander. By adding grated carrots, zucchini and chopped onion you could have a meal in a pan in minutes. Serve with a green salad.

Cacciatora Casserole

1 can (410 g) tomatoes,
 chopped
1 medium onion, sliced
2 large cloves garlic,
 chopped
¼ cup dry sherry
1 tablespoon tomato paste★
1 large bayleaf
1 cup cooked wholemeal
 macaroni shapes
500 g steamed mixed
 vegetables
1 cup button mushrooms,
 sliced
¼ cup water
1 dessertspoon cornflour
1 dessertspoon finely
 chopped parsley

Combine first 6 ingredients in pan, cover and simmer 15 minutes. Place macaroni, mixed vegetables and mushrooms in casserole dish. Remove bayleaf from sauce in pan and pour sauce over vegetables, lightly folding through to gently mix. Place covered dish in moderate oven, 200°C (400°F) to reheat — if vegetables are hot, 10 minutes; if cold, 15 minutes. Remove dish from oven and, if desired, thicken sauce with water and cornflour mix, folding through gently to avoid vegetable breakdown. Cover and replace in oven further 5 minutes. Serve with sprinkling of parsley.

Variation
Replace macaroni with cooked dried beans (legumes).

Serving suggestion
Serve with Crunchy Vegetarian Salad (page 13).

★ See cooking notes.

Serves 4

Stewed Tomato and Onion

2 large tomatoes, chopped
1 tablespoon Tomato
 Magic★
1 medium onion, finely
 chopped
1 clove garlic, chopped
1 tablespoon chopped fresh
 coriander

Place all ingredients, except coriander, in saucepan. Cover and gently heat, stirring occasionally until cooked — about 15 minutes. Sprinkle with coriander and serve.

Serving suggestions
Serve on toast for breakfast. Use as a filling for Jacket Baked Potatoes (page 29), or as an accompaniment with:

- Steamed chicken breast
- Grilled fish
- Bean and Spinach Loaf (page 37)
- Crunchy Vegetarian Pie (page 33)
- Spicy Vegetable Patties (page 36)

* See cooking notes.

Brussels Sprouts and Mushrooms Italian

1 can (410 g) tomatoes,
  chopped
2 cloves garlic, chopped
1 small onion, cut into rings
1 tablespoon tomato paste*
½ teaspoon oregano
½ teaspoon basil
2 bay leaves
250 g Brussels sprouts
200 g cultured mushrooms,
  roughly chopped
coriander sprigs for garnish

Place all ingredients except sprouts, mushrooms and coriander in pan and simmer 1 hour. If sprouts are large, halve or quarter. Add to sauce in pan. Cover and simmer until just cooked — about 10 minutes. Then add mushrooms. Cook another few minutes. Remove bay leaves. Garnish with sprigs of coriander. Serve immediately.

Serving suggestion
Serve as an entree with wholemeal pasta shells, or as a luncheon dish with wholemeal pasta shells and a green salad. Serve as part of main course with Jacket Baked Potato (page 29) (brushed with yoghurt while cooking), steamed choko and carrots.

Variation
Sprouts may be steamed whole, and sauce with mushrooms may be spooned over. Broccoli or cauliflower may replace sprouts.

* See cooking notes.

Serves 4

Pepita, Bean and Vegetable Delight

1 small bunch spinach
1 large carrot, grated
1 large zucchini, grated
1 medium onion, grated
½ cup chopped mint
2 cups cooked beans
   (legumes)
½ cup pepitas
2 tablespoons tomato paste★
1 egg white
tomato slices for topping

Trim long stalks from spinach. Wash, chop and steam leaves for 3-4 minutes. Drain excess water and mix spinach with all other ingredients except tomato slices. Pack firmly into shallow oven dish. Top with tomato slices. Cover with lid or foil and bake at 200°C (400°F) for 30 minutes. Remove cover and bake further 15 minutes.

Serving suggestion
Serve with steamed pumpkin and snow peas, or green salad.
Variation
After removing cover, top with a Yoghurt Toast Topping (page 82) and cook uncovered further 15 minutes, or until toast is crisp and brown. Serve immediately.

N.B. Pepitas are Mexican pumpkin seeds, available at health food stores.

★ See cooking notes.

Serves 6

Spicy Vegetable Patties

1 packet 'Spicy Vegetable
   Casserole'★
1 cup left-over vegetables,
   mashed
1 cup cooked brown rice
1 egg white

Place casserole mix in saucepan with 2 cups water. Stir and heat until water is absorbed, adding a little more water if vegetables are not soft. Add vegetables, rice and egg white. Shape into patties. Bake on a non-stick tray in moderate oven 200°C (400°F), or cook in non-stick pan on cooktop until heated and nicely browned.

Variation
Substitute cooked mashed beans (legumes) or cooked cold lentils (brown) for rice.

Patties may be coated in Yoghurt Topping Crumbs (page 82).

Serving suggestion
Serve hot with steamed vegetables, accompanied by Stewed Tomato and Onion (page 34), or cold for sandwiches and salads.

* See cooking notes.

Serves 4

Bean and Spinach Loaf

4 cups cooked mixed beans
   (legumes)
1 cup soft breadcrumbs
1 medium onion, finely
   chopped
½ cup chopped parsley
2 cloves garlic, chopped
1 teaspoon paprika
1 egg white
1 small bunch spinach,
   chopped, steamed and
   drained
fine breadcrumbs for
   coating

Place all ingredients, except spinach and fine breadcrumbs, in food processor and process until smooth.

Place in large sheet of plastic food wrap or greaseproof paper on workbench and cover evenly with fine breadcrumbs. Place mixture on breadcrumbs and flatten to about 1 cm (½ inch) thick, in an oblong shape, and spread spinach over. Take two corners at same end of sheet and lift to roll mixture (as in making Swiss roll cake). When rolled, place on non-stick oven tray and bake at 200°C (400°F) for about 30 minutes.

Variation
Loaf may be rolled in Yoghurt Topping Crumbs (page 82).
Serving suggestion
Serve hot with vegetables or cold with salad.

Serves 6

Vegetarian Goulash With Dumplings

1 can (410 g) tomatoes
1 large onion, sliced into
  rings
1 medium green capsicum,
  sliced
500 g bite-size raw mixed
  vegetables
1 cup chicken stock
3 teaspoons tomato paste*
1 level teaspoon paprika
1 bay leaf
¼ teaspoon nutmeg
1 tablespoon cornflour
¼ cup water

Dumplings
2 cups self-raising
  wholemeal flour
¼ cup finely chopped fresh
  parsley
1 small cup skim milk

Place tomatoes, onion, capsicum, vegetables, stock, tomato paste, paprika, bay leaf and nutmeg in a large pan or saucepan. Bring to the boil. Reduce heat, cover and simmer 30 minutes. Remove bay leaf and thicken with cornflour mixed with water.

To make dumplings, combine flour and parsley. Add milk all at once and mix well. Drop teaspoonsful of mixture into pan with goulash, spacing well around the edge because dumplings will double in size when cooked. Cover pan. Simmer for 15 minutes. Flip dumplings over and cover again to cook further 5 minutes.

Serving suggestion
Spoon ½ cup of Sour Cream Dressing over vegetables, sprinkling with a little chopped fresh parsley. Serve immediately, accompanied by a side salad.

* See cooking notes

Serves 4

Variations of Versatile Mushrooms

4 large cultured
  mushrooms, wiped clean
  and stalks removed

Fill mushroom caps with any of the following, and bake on a non-stick tray, loosely covered with foil, for 15 minutes in a moderate oven 175°C (375°F).
- ½ quantity of Herb and Breadcrumb Seasoning (page 74).
- Lemon juice and chopped chives.
- Chopped tomato and chopped shallots.
- Chopped tomato and chopped fresh herbs.
- Any suitable leftovers.

Serving suggestions
Serve hot as a side vegetable, or hot on Savoury Toasties (page 75) as an entree. Also serve hot on Savoury Toast accompanied by Crunchy Vegetarian Salad (page 13) as a luncheon dish.

If desired, use smaller mushrooms and serve hot on small pieces of Savoury Toast as canapes.

N.B. Do not overcook because mushrooms will collapse.

Serves 4

Vegetable and Chick Pea Curry

---

1 medium onion, chopped
2 cloves garlic, chopped
2 teaspoons curry powder
½ teaspoon cummin powder
½ teaspoon garam masala
2 cups chicken or vegetable stock
1 medium potato, thickly sliced
1 medium carrot, thickly sliced
1 cup broccoli florets
1 cup cauliflower florets
1 cup cooked chick peas
2 tablespoons tomato paste★
1 cup water
heaped tablespoon cornflour

Place a little water in a large frying pan. Add onion, garlic, curry, cummin and garam masala. Stir over low heat until onion has softened slightly. Add stock, potato and carrot. Cover and simmer over medium heat 15 minutes. Add broccoli, cauliflower and chick peas. Cover and cook further 10 minutes. Add tomato paste. Mix cornflour with cup of water until smooth. Then add to pan, stirring gently until curry thickens. Allow to cool 3 minutes more.

Serving suggestion
Serve hot with steamed brown rice, and side dishes of Cucumber Dressing (page 80) and Cold Tomato Capsicum Relish (page 80).

Variation
Any vegetable may be substituted or added, e.g. mushrooms, zucchini, beans, peas. Sultanas may also be added.

★ See cooking notes.

Serves 2

Vegetarian Chilli Beans

1 can (410 g) tomatoes
1 medium onion, chopped
3 cloves garlic, finely
  chopped
1 dessertspoon Tomato
  Magic*
¼ teaspoon ground cummin
  seed
½ teaspoon dried oregano
  leaves
1 rounded teaspoon chilli
  powder
2½ cups cooked red kidney
  beans

Place all ingredients except kidney beans in saucepan. Bring to boil over medium heat. Reduce heat, cover, and simmer 30 minutes. Add kidney beans, cover and simmer 15 minutes.

Serving suggestion
Serve as an entree with toast, or as a luncheon dish with toast and salad. Spoon over steamed vegetables or use leftover amounts to fill Jacket Baked Potatoes (page 29), capsicums, eggplant, tomatoes and zucchini.

N.B. This dish is ideal for freezing.

* See cooking notes.

Serves 2

Zucchini Geska

4 medium zucchini
1 medium tomato, finely
  chopped
1 small onion, finely
  chopped
1 teaspoon Tomato Magic
  (Italian style)*
fresh breadcrumbs
Geska cheese
chopped coriander or
  parsley

Trim ends of zucchini and slice lengthways. Remove flesh (save for stock) leaving a cavity for filling. Mix together tomato, onion and Tomato Magic. Fill zucchini and place breadcrumbs over. Then sprinkle with Geska cheese. Place on baking tray and cook in moderate oven 200°C (400°F) 30 minutes. Sprinkle coriander or parsley over and serve immediately.

Serving suggestion
Serve with Jacket Baked Potatoes (page 29) with Sour Cream Dressing (page 80) and chives, and steamed pumpkin and broccoli.

Variation
Any leftover filling is good topped with breadcrumbs and Geska cheese.

* See cooking notes.

Serves 4

Vegetarian Pizza

---

1 large round of flat
   wholemeal Lebanese
   bread (low salt)
2 tablespoons tomato paste*
1 teaspoon dried oregano
   leaves
1 teaspoon dried basil leaves
1 teaspoon dried granulated
   garlic
½ cup finely chopped onion
½ cup mushrooms, roughly
   chopped
½ cup green capsicum,
   finely chopped
Geska cheese

Cover bread with tomato paste. Sprinkle with herbs and garlic. Then sprinkle with onions, mushrooms, capsicum and, finally, a generous sprinkling of Geska cheese. Place on a flat tray and bake at 200°C (400°F) about 15 minutes.

Serving suggestion
Serve immediately with green salad for luncheon.

Variation
Using the above ingredients, any of the following may be added — pineapple pieces, grated carrot, grated zucchini, chopped celery.

N.B. Wholemeal Lebanese bread comes in large or small rounds. Use large for luncheon and small for entree or snacks. Pritikin* bread may be substituted.

* See cooking notes.

Per person

PASTA AND RICE

To Cook Brown Rice

The rice used in the recipes in this book, is always brown rice because the fibre, and the vitamin and mineral rich hull has not been discarded. It is a good idea, before cooking, to rid the rice of any dirt or dust by rinsing in a colander under running water. This will ensure that nothing detracts from the clean nutty flavour.

Evaporation method
Equal quantities of rice and water (or other liquids)
2 cups rice
2 cups water
Place rice and water in a heavy-based saucepan and cover. Bring to the boil, then turn heat right down to very low and allow to cook 35-40 minutes. Do not lift lid or 'fork through', otherwise the network of little passageways allowing the steam to escape and rice to cook evenly will be disturbed, making the rice sticky instead of light and fluffy. If you are worried about burning the rice, place a simmer ring or mat under the saucepan.

Boiling method
Two-thirds fill your largest size saucepan with water. Bring to the boil. Whilst boiling, pour in 2 cups of rice. Boil rapidly, uncovered, for 35 minutes. Drain in colander and serve.

Storage and reheating
Cooked rice may be stored in an airtight container in the refrigerator.

To reheat, put cold cooked rice in colander and place under running hot water, forking through for 1 minute. Place colander over a saucepan of boiling water, cover rice and steam 10 minutes. Uncover, fork through and cook 2 or 3 minutes.

N.B. When reheating, the water in the saucepan should be below the rice level. If rice is to be kept hot for a long period, lower the heat, cover rice and fork through occasionally.

Flavoured Rice

It is best to use the evaporation method to make flavoured rice. Each recipe uses 2 cups of raw rice and 2 cups of liquid.

Lemon Rice *see Flavoured Rice* (above)

1¾ cups water
¼ cup lemon juice
1 teaspoon grated lemon rind
¼ teaspoon turmeric

Serve with Saucy Jewfish Cutlets (page 53).

Orange Rice *see Flavoured Rice* (above)

2 cups orange juice

Use for Orange Rice Cream (page 66).

Apple Rice *see Flavoured Rice* (page 43)

---

2 cups unsweetened apple juice

Use for Brown Rice and Apple Salad (page 17).

Tomato Rice *see Flavoured Rice* (page 43)

---

2 cups tomato juice

Serve with steamed vegetables.

Garlic Rice *see Flavoured Rice* (page 43)

---

2 cups water
Desired quantity of garlic cloves, chopped. (Vary according to taste.)

Serve with Chinese Vegetables (page 24).

Spinach Cannelloni

---

9 cannelloni tubes
1 quantity of Basic Tomato Sauce (page 83)

Thaw and drain excess water from spinach. Mix filling ingredients in food processor. Fill pasta tubes. Allow 3 tubes per person.

Pour a small amount of tomato sauce into shallow dish so that it just covers the bottom. Place filled tubes

44

Filling
1 packet frozen spinach
200 g ricotta cheese*
1 pinch nutmeg
1 egg white

in dish. Then pour the remainder of sauce over the tubes. Cover dish with lid or foil and bake at 190°C (350°F) for 45 minutes.

Serving suggestion
Sprinkle with Geska cheese and accompany with steamed broccoli and carrots, or Crunchy Vegetarian Salad (page 13).

* See cooking notes

Serves 3

Salmon Rice Cake

---

1 can (210 g) salmon
2 cups cooked brown rice (cold)
1 small onion, finely chopped
½ small red capsicum, finely chopped
½ cup finely chopped chives
1 tablespoon lemon juice
1 tablespoon Sour Cream Dressing (page 80)
1 egg white
parsley for garnish

Drain salmon and separate with a fork. Place all ingredients except Sour Cream Dressing in bowl and mix together with a fork. Gently fold Sour Cream Dressing and egg white through. Press into a spring-form pan, or a non-stick cake tin or pudding bowl. Place in refrigerator and chill at least one hour. Carefully turn out onto serving dish and reshape if necessary.

Serving suggestion
Place endive leaves and halved cherry tomatoes around edge of dish. Top the cake with a little Sour Cream Dressing and a parsley sprig.

Variation
Fresh cooked fish or shredded steamed chicken could replace salmon.

Serves 4

45

Vegetable Lasagna

wholemeal instant lasagna
   sheets
6 large spinach leaves,
   washed and chopped
1 large zucchini, grated
1 large carrot, grated
1 quantity Basic Tomato
   Sauce (page 83)
Geska cheese

Place spinach, zucchini and carrot in frying pan, with a little water to stop it sticking. Cover and cook about 3 or 4 minutes. Drain well.

Into a non-stick, oblong, baking dish about 28 cm x 18 cm (11 x 7 inches) spoon a layer of sauce. Cover with a pasta layer. Then vegetables and more sauce. Repeat layers, ending with pasta, then sauce. Sprinkle with Geska cheese. Lightly cover with foil and bake at 200°C (400°F) about 45 minutes, until knife cuts cleanly through pasta.

Serving suggestion
Serve with green salad and hot Herb Rolls (page 78).

Variation
Top with layer of Basic White Sauce (page 79) and sprinkle generously with Geska cheese and breadcrumbs.

Serves 4

Dry Fried Rice

1 medium onion, chopped
2 medium zucchini, grated
1 medium carrot, grated
1 cup mushrooms, chopped
1 teaspoon grated root
   ginger
1 large clove garlic, chopped
2 cups cooked rice
1 tablespoon tamari
½ cup chopped shallots

Sprinkle a little water in a non-stick pan and place in the first six ingredients. Stir to mix, then cover and cook about 2 minutes. Uncover, add rice and tamari, and cook a few minutes to heat the rice, stirring gently to prevent scorching. Lastly, add shallots and serve immediately.

Serving suggestion
Serve with Fish Stirfry (page 54).

CHICKEN AND FISH

Golden Chicken with Apricot

4 chicken breasts, skin and
   bone removed
2 cups chicken stock
½ cup Apricot Spread
   (page 83)
1 dessertspoon mild
   mustard*
3 shallots, chopped
1 dessertspon cornflour
¼ cup water

Add chicken to stock. Cover and simmer, turning chicken occasionally, for 15 minutes. Combine Apricot Spread with mustard, mixing well. Then add with the shallots to the pan, stirring well. Cover and simmer further 15-20 minutes, until chicken is tender. Thicken with cornflour and water.

Serving suggestion
Served with mashed potatoes with chopped fresh parsley and chopped raw onion, Ginger Cabbage (page 22) and steamed pumpkin or carrots.

* Mustard is not generally accepted, but I have used Hains Natural Stoneground Mustard* — all natural, no preservatives, salt or chemicals. This product is American and may be found in specialty shops or delicatessens.

Serves 4

Chicken in Orange Sauce

2 chicken breasts, skinned
1 cup orange juice
1 clove garlic, chopped
1 tablespoon tamari
½ cup dry sherry
1 orange, peeled and sliced
1 cup button mushrooms,
    thickly chopped
extra ¼ cup orange juice
1 dessertspoon cornflour

Lightly slash chicken breasts to avoid curling. Place in casserole dish. Mix cup of orange juice, garlic, tamari and dry sherry, and pour over chicken. Place orange slices on top. Cover and bake about 45 minutes at 180°C (375°F). Remove cover and add mushrooms. Use mixed juice and cornflour to thicken as desired. (Use more or less juice or cornflour to taste.) Cover and replace in oven a few minutes until cornflour is completely absorbed. Garnish with fresh coriander or parsley sprigs.

Serving suggestion
Serve with dry baked potatoes and steamed fresh green beans, finely cut.

N.B. This recipe may be slowly cooked in a covered pan on cooktop, or in a frypan.

Serves 2

Chicken Parcels

1 chicken breast, skin and
    bone removed

Flatten breast with a meat mallet. Place any of the following fillings on the breast. Roll up and secure with toothpicks. Place in a casserole dish or frypan with a little water. Cover and bake about 45 minutes on moderate heat 200°C (400°F). Remove toothpicks and serve.
Fillings
• Minted Spinach (page 21)
• Herb and Breadcrumb Seasoning (page 74)

Serving suggestion for both
Serve with Stewed Tomato and Onion (page 34), dry baked potatoes, pumpkin, steamed beans and steamed cauliflower. A little Geska cheese may be sprinkled over cauliflower.

Variation
Rub chicken with garlic. Fill with a little grated ginger and chopped shallots. Cook as above, but while cooking add 1 cup chicken stock and 2 teaspoons tamari. When cooked, add a little cornflour mixed with water to thicken sauce.

Serving suggestion
Serve with brown rice, steamed carrots and broccoli or snow peas.

Per person

Chicken Casserole

---

4 chicken breasts, skin and
  bone removed
1 medium onion, sliced into
  rings
2 celery stalks, roughly
  chopped
2 medium carrots, sliced
2 medium potatoes, diced
1 level teaspoon mixed
  herbs
4 cups chicken stock
1 cup button mushrooms,
  halved
1 level tablespoon cornflour
¼ cup skim milk

Place all ingredients, except mushrooms, cornflour and milk, in covered casserole and bake on moderate heat, 200°C (400°F) for 1 hour. Add mushrooms, then mix cornflour with milk and use to thicken sauce. Return to heat for further 3 minutes.

Serving suggestion
Serve with brown rice and steamed green vegetables.

Variations
Curry powder may be added to taste. Half a cup of dry white wine may be added if desired.

Serves 4

Tarragon Chicken

4 chicken breasts, skinned
4 medium tomatoes,
  coarsely chopped
1 large onion, sliced
2 teaspoons dried tarragon
  leaves

Place all in non-stick pan with one cup water. Cover and cook over moderate to low heat about 25 minutes, moving ingredients around occasionally to avoid sticking.

Variation
Chopped mushrooms and zucchini could be added in the last 5 minutes of cooking.

Serving suggestion
Serve with Crunchy Vegetarian Salad (page 13).

Serves 4

Keith's Teriyaki Mullet

2 large mullet fillets,
  skinned

Marinade
2 cloves garlic, finely
  chopped or grated
1 teaspoon root ginger,
  finely grated
4 tablespoons tamari
2 tablespoons lemon juice
1 cup chicken stock

Mix marinade ingredients and allow fish to marinate at least ½ hour (longer is better). Cover grill tray with foil. Spray with non-stick spray. Grill fillets 5-10 minutes, depending on size. Brush marinade over while cooking. Heat remaining marinade and pour over fish when serving.

Serving suggestion
Serve hot with steamed brown rice and steamed spinach. Double sauce quantity to pour over rice and spinach.
Serve cold with Crunchy Vegetarian Salad (page 13).

Variation
This marinade may be used for other fish or chicken.

N.B. Fishmongers will clean, skin and fillet fish. Mullet must be very fresh and must be deep sea mullet.

Serves 2

Schnapper with Asparagus

1 medium schnapper (about 1.5 kg)

Seasoning
1 can (340 g) asparagus, drained and mashed
1 cup soft breadcrumbs
1 small onion, finely chopped
¼ cup chopped chives
sprinkling Geska cheese

Slash fish lightly 2 or 3 times each side. Combine seasoning ingredients and place in cavity of fish. Place fish in covered baking pan or wrapped and sealed in foil. Cook at 200°C (400°F) 20-30 minutes.

Serving suggestion
Serve with Potato Chips (page 28), steamed broccoli, carrots and lemon White Sauce (page 79).

Serves 4

Rice and Herb Schnapper

1 medium schnapper (about 1½ kg)

Seasoning
1 cup cooked brown rice
1 cup button mushrooms, halved
¼ cup finely chopped fresh lemon thyme

Slash fish lightly 2 or 3 times each side. Mix seasoning ingredients and place in cavity of fish. Place fish in covered baking pan, or wrap in foil, and bake in moderate oven 200°C (400°F) about 30 minutes.

Serving suggestion
Serve immediately with Ginger Spinach (page 23).

Serves 4

Baked Schnapper with Ginger

1 medium schnapper
  (about 1.5 kg)

Sauce
1 garlic clove, chopped
1 teaspoon grated ginger
4 shallots, chopped
3 tablespoons tamari
3 tablespoons water
2 tablespoons cornflour

Slash fish 2 or 3 times lightly on both sides. Place fish, on enough foil to make into a parcel, in a shallow baking pan. Combine other ingredients and pour over fish. Bring edges of foil together to make a sealed parcel. Bake in moderate oven 200°C (400°F) about 30 minutes.

Serving suggestion
Serve with hot brown rice, steamed broccoli and carrots.

Variations
If more sauce is desired, use marinade from Keith's Teriyaki Mullet (page 50) to pour over rice.
    Fish Parcels may be cooked on barbecue.

Serves 4

Mixed Herbs and Lemon Schnapper

1 medium schnapper
  (about 1.5 kg)
½ cup lemon juice
½ cup water
dried mixed herbs

Slash fish lightly 2 or 3 times each side. Place fish in baking pan. Mix juice and water. Pour into cavity and over fish. Sprinkle both sides of fish generously with mixed herbs. Cover, seal and bake at 200°C (400°F) about 30 minutes, or until cooked.

Serving suggestion
Serve with Potato Chips (page 28) and steamed green vegetables.

Variation
Omit mixed herbs.

Serves 4

Mixed Herbs and Lemon Schnapper
(page 52)
Saucy Jewfish Cutlets (page 53)
Spinach Cannelloni (page 44)

Garlic Schnapper

1 medium schnapper
  (about 1.5 kg)
whole garlic cloves

Slash fish 2 or 3 times on each side. Place on foil and fill cavity with as many garlic cloves as desired. Bring edges of foil together to make a parcel, and bake at 200°C (400°F) about 30 minutes, or until cooked. Remove garlic, and serve with Chinese Vegetables (page 24).

Serves 4

Saucy Jewfish Cutlets

4 jewfish cutlets
1 cup lemon juice
1 cup water

Sauce
1 can (410 g) tomatoes
1 small onion, chopped
1 stick celery, chopped
1 tablespoon chopped
  coriander
coriander sprigs

Place tomatoes, onion and celery in blender, and puree. Pour puree into saucepan, cover and heat gently, stirring occasionally. Combine lemon juice with one cup of water. Pour into a large pan and gently poach fish for about 10 minutes, carefully turning after 5 minutes. Cooking time will depend on thickness of cutlets. When fish is cooked, remove sauce from heat and add the coriander. Place fish on serving plate and spoon sauce across the centre, topping with a coriander sprig.

Variation
Fish may be oven baked. Halve the quantity of lemon juice and water and seal the baking dish with foil. It is not necessary to turn fish over if using this method.

Serving suggestion
Serve with Crunchy Vegetarian Salad (page 13), or with Potato and Herb Layer (page 30), using fresh chives and steamed broccoli.

Fish Stirfry

Marinade
2 tablespoons dry sherry
2 tablespoons tamari
2 tablespoons water
1 tablespoon cornflour

500 g firm boneless fish
½ cup water
1 medium onion, sliced
1 medium zucchini, thinly
  sliced
1 teaspoon grated ginger
2 cloves garlic, chopped
250 g mung beansprouts
½ red capsicum, chopped
½ cup chicken stock
1 tablespoon tamari
2 teaspoons cornflour

Cut fish into bite-size pieces and marinade in sherry, tamari, water and cornflour mix, at least 30 minutes.

In a non-stick wok or frying pan, pour ½ cup water. Then add onion, zucchini, ginger and garlic. Over a medium heat, stir for 2 minutes. Add fish, beansprouts and capsicum. Cover and cook further 2 minutes. Combine chicken stock, tamari and cornflour, and add to fish and vegetables, stirring gently until heated. Serve immediately.

Serving suggestion
Serve with steamed rice or Dry Fried Rice (page 46).

Serves 4

Salmon Rissoles

1 can (210 g) salmon (no
  salt), drained
1 medium onion, finely
  chopped
½ cup finely chopped celery
2 cups cooked cold mashed
  potato
1 egg white
1 tablespoon lemon juice
¼ cup chopped fresh
  parsley
fine breadcrumbs for
  coating

Place all ingredients except breadcrumbs into bowl. Mix well. Form into rissoles and coat with breadcrumbs. Place on a non-stick tray in a moderate oven 200°C (400°F). Turning once or twice, bake about 30 minutes, or until lightly browned and crisp.

Serving suggestion
Serve hot with Chips (page 28) and steamed fresh green peas and carrots with Lemon Parsley Sauce (page 79).
Serve cold with salad.
Make into small balls instead of rissoles. Bake and serve hot or cold as appetisers.

Variation
Remove top and centre from Pritikin* breadrolls. Fill cavity with salmon mixture. Bake in foil 20 minutes. Remove foil, place top on roll, brush with low-fat natural yoghurt, and cook further 5 minutes. Serve immediately.

N.B. Cooked rice or fresh breadcrumbs could replace mashed potato.

Serves 4

Tuna and Vegi Bake

3 large potatoes
skim milk
1 can (180 g) water-packed
   tuna
juice of 1 lemon
2 zucchini, sliced
1 green capsicum, sliced
2 tomatoes, cut into chunks
1 medium onion, cut into
   rings
4 large cultivated
   mushrooms, sliced
water (about 1 tablespoon)
1 tablespoon fresh chopped
   coriander
Geska cheese

Steam and mash potatoes with a little skim milk. Drain tuna, place in bowl and flake. Pour lemon juce over tuna and allow to stand. Place zucchini, capsicum, tomatoes, onions and mushrooms in a non-stick pan with about 1 tablespoon of water. Cover and cook over a medium heat about 5 minutes, stirring occasionally to prevent catching. Take pan off heat and stir tuna and coriander through gently. Pour into ovenproof dish and cover with mashed potato, then sprinkle with Geska cheese and bake about 15 minutes in a moderate oven 200°C (400°F) until heated through.

Serving suggestion
Serve as a luncheon dish with salad, or a main dish with other vegetables.

Variation
Replace tuna with salmon.

Serves 4

Salmon and Vegi Loaf

1 quantity Salmon Rissoles
  mixture (page 54)
2 medium carrots, grated
1 large tomato, sliced
¼ cup finely chopped chives
2 large zucchini, grated
breadcrumbs

Line a loaf tin or ovenproof dish with non-stick baking paper. Place half salmon mixture in tin or dish, followed by the carrots, tomato, chives, zucchini and, finally, the remainder of the salmon mixture. Press down gently. Sprinkle with breadcrumbs and bake in moderate oven 200°C (400°F) about 30 minutes. Remove from oven and allow to rest 5 minutes. Place a plate or board over tin and, holding both, turn upside down to release loaf in one piece. Remove paper. Place serving dish over loaf and, holding both plates, turn the loaf back right way up to serve.

Serving suggestion
Serve hot with steamed snow peas and Potato Salad served hot (page 11).
Serve cold with Fresh Green Herb Salad (page 18).

Tuna and Savoury Toast

1 small onion, finely
  chopped
1 stick celery, finely
  chopped
4 tablespoons of water
1½ cups skim milk
2 teaspoons cornflour
1 can (180 g) tuna, drained
1 teaspoon grated lemon
  rind
1 teaspoon lemon juice
1 tablespoon fresh chopped
  parsley
grated carrot
2 pieces Savoury Tomato on
  Toast (page 2)

In a medium saucepan, place onion, celery, and 2 tablespoons of the water. Saute 2 or 3 minutes. Add milk and, when nearly boiling, thicken with cornflour mixed in remaining water. Add tuna, lemon rind, juice and parsley. Stir gently a few more minutes.

Serving suggestion
Serve in a warmed dish with carrot sprinkled over, and arrange triangles of Savoury Toast around tuna.

Variation
Replace tuna with salmon.

Serves 2

56

DESSERTS

Apple Pie

1 Three Flours Pastry Case
   (page 77)
4 large apples
½ cup water
½ cup sultanas
4 teaspoons jam*
cinnamon
topping pieces (page 82)

Peel, slice and stew apples in ½ cup water in a covered saucepan. When cooked, remove from heat, add sultanas and mix. Place hot apples in pastry case. Spread small portions of jam over apples, and sprinkle with cinnamon. Spoon topping mix over and spread to cover (see page 82). Cook in moderate oven 175°C (375°F) for 10 minutes.

Serving suggestion
Serve hot or cold with Dessert Cream (page 58) or Vanilla Ice Cream (page 61).

* See cooking notes.

Baked Custard

2 tablespoons raisins
3 cups water
1½ cups skim milk powder
1 teaspoon vanilla essence
½ teaspoon lemon rind
3 egg whites, beaten
nutmeg

Place 1 cup water in a blender with the raisins. Process until liquidised. Then add remainder of water, lemon rind, essence and milk powder. Process until well blended. Pour blended mix onto beaten egg whites and gently mix. Pour into oven dish and sprinkle with nutmeg. Place dish in pan of water and bake at 175°C (350°F) for 1 hour.

Serves 4

Dessert Cream

ricotta cheese or cottage
  cheese*
skim milk
vanilla essence

Blend ricotta with milk and a little vanilla essence to desired consistency. Add more or less milk depending whether a pouring or a firmer cream is required.

Variation
Any fruit or juices may be added or substituted for milk, e.g. orange rind and juice, or strawberries, etc.

* See cooking notes about cheese.

N.B. If using cottage cheese, flavour with mashed banana and a little orange juice to counteract the slightly sour taste of the cheese.

Any quantity

Crepes

1 cup plain wholemeal flour
1¼ cups skim milk
4 egg whites, stiffly beaten

Mix milk with flour until smooth. Carefully fold in egg whites. Heat a non-stick frying pan (preferably a heavy one). Pour in some of the batter, rotating the pan to distribute it evenly. It should be as thin as possible. Flip the crepe over when bubbles appear, to cook other side.

Sweet fillings
• Hot stewed apple, a few sultanas, a few teaspoons of jam* and a sprinkling of cinnamon.
• Mashed banana, heated with a little orange juice and with a little passionfruit mixed through.
• Strawberries mixed with a litttle Dessert Cream (above).

Serving suggestion
Serve with Ice Cream (page 61) or Dessert Cream
(page 58).

Savoury fillings
• Fresh mushrooms and onion rings, sauteed in a
little lemon juice.
• Vegetarian Chilli Beans (page 40).
• Basic White Sauce (page 79) with cooked chicken or
fish added.

Serving suggestion
Spoon extra filling over crepe and sprinkle liberally
with chopped fresh herbs, such as chives, coriander or
parsley.

★ See cooking notes.

Three Flours Pancake

**1½ cups flour mix (page 77)
cold water or fruit juice**

Combine flour with water or fruit juice to make a thick
pouring consistency. Heat a non-stick pan and pour in
a quarter of the batter, spreading thinly. Place filling
to one side of the pancake. Fold other side over to meet
the edge and press to seal. Cook 1 minute, then carefully turn over to cook other side. Serve immediately.

Variation
Spice or dried herbs may be added to flour.

Suggested fillings
Mashed ripe bananas
Hot stewed apples with sultanas

Serving suggestion
Spoon fresh squeezed orange juice over when serving.

Makes 4

Pikelets

1 cup wholemeal self-raising
   flour
¾ cup skim milk
4 egg whites, stiffly beaten

Mix milk with flour until smooth. Carefully fold in egg whites. Heat a non-stick frying pan (preferably a heavy one). Spoon in portions of the batter. Flip pikelets over when bubbles appear, to cook other side. Spread with a little jam★ and Dessert Cream (page 58).

★ See cooking notes.

Carob Ice Cream

½ cup raisins
1 cup hot water
1 cup cold water
1 teaspoon vanilla essence
3 rounded tablespoons
   carob powder
225 g powdered skim milk
2 teaspoons gelatine,
   dissolved in hot water

Place raisins in blender with hot water. Allow to soak 15 minutes, then process to liquefy. Add 1 cup cold water, vanilla essence and carob powder. Process, then add milk powder, and process again. Finally, add gelatine, processing to mix. Freeze in shallow pan until just firm (not hard). Beat in a chilled bowl until mixture doubles in volume. (An electric beater is best.) Refreeze in a covered container.

Serving suggestion
Serve with pears poached in a little orange juice, or with strawberries and kiwi fruit.

Pineapple Ice Cream

1 can (440 g) unsweetened
   pineapple pieces
⅔ cup water
225 g skim milk powder
2 teaspoons gelatine

Place pineapple pieces with juice and water in blender and process to liquefy. Add milk powder and process. Dissolve gelatine in a little hot water, add to mixture and process. Freeze in shallow pan until firm (not hard). Place in a chilled bowl and, using (preferably) an electric mixer, beat until doubled in volume. Refreeze in a covered container.

Christmas Ice Cream Cake

½ cup raisins
1 cup hot water
1 cup cold water
3 heaped tablespoons carob
    powder
1 teaspoon vanilla essence
250 g powdered skim milk
2 teaspoons gelatine,
    dissolved in hot water
1 cup mixed fruit
3 tablespoons rum

Place raisins in blender with hot water. Soak 15 minutes then process to liquefy. Add 1 cup cold water, carob powder and vanilla. Process again, then add skim milk. Process, add gelatine, process and freeze in a shallow uncovered pan until firm (not hard). Beat in a chilled bowl until doubled in volume. (An electric beater is best.) Line a Christmas pudding container with foil or plastic wrap. Pour mixture in, cover and place in freezer.

Plump fruit and rum in microwave 1 minute, or in small covered saucepan slowly. Set aside. When ice cream starts to firm, fold fruit through and, if necessary, stir gently occasionally to stop fruit settling on the bottom. When serving, uncover bowl, place a chilled plate over and tip out. Remove foil or plastic carefully, and place a piece of holly, or other decoration on top. Fresh fruit may be placed around the base, if desired.

N.B. The alcohol is cooked out of the rum when plumping.

Vanilla Ice Cream

¼ cup raisins
1 cup hot water
1 cup cold water
1 teaspoon vanilla essence
225 g skim milk powder
2 level teaspoons gelatine

Place raisins in hot water in blender and allow to stand 15 minutes to soften raisins. Process to liquefy the raisins, then add cold water, vanilla, and milk powder, and process again till well mixed. Dissolve gelatine in a little hot water, add to mixture and process again. Freeze in a shallow pan until just firm (not hard). Place ice cream in chilled bowl and beat until doubled in volume, light and fluffy (preferably with an electric mixer). Pour into an ice cream container, cover and refreeze.

Rhubarb Ice Cream

¼ **cup raisins**
1 **cup hot water**
2 **cups Rhubarb and Fruit**
 Casserole (page 63)
225 **g skim milk powder**
2 **level teaspoons gelatine**

Place raisins and hot water in blender and allow to stand 15 minutes to soften raisins. Process to liquefy. Add rhubarb and fruit mix: process. Add milk powder and process again. Soften gelatine in a little hot water, add to blender and process. Pour into a shallow pan and freeze until just firm (not hard). Place mixture in a chilled bowl and beat (preferably with an electric mixer) until doubled in volume. Pour into an ice cream container, cover and refreeze.

Rhubarb and Apple

500 **g rhubarb**
1 **cup chopped dates**
2 **red apples, peeled and**
 sliced
⅔ **cup water**

Trim, wash and chop rhubarb into chunks. Place all ingredients in stainless steel, glass or enamel saucepan, placing the lid so that it almost covers but allowing steam to escape. Cook gently until rhubarb is soft, adding a little more water if necessary to prevent catching.

Serving suggestion
Serve hot or cold with Dessert Cream (page 58) or Vanilla Ice Cream (page 61).

Instant Cream

1 **can low-fat evaporated**
 milk, chilled

Using a blender or wand, process milk thoroughly. If milk is cold enough, the volume should double.

Variation
After processing, gently fold through chopped strawberries or grated orange rind.

Carob Custard

½ cup raisins, softened in
enough hot water to cover
2 cups skim milk
2 heaped tablespoons carob
powder
½ teaspoon vanilla essence
2 rounded tablespoons
cornflour

Place raisins, 1½ cups of water, carob powder and essence into blender and process to blend smoothly. Pour into saucepan and bring nearly to the boil. Mix cornflour with remaining milk till smooth. Remove saucepan from heat. Add cornflour mixture. Stir quickly and well, then return to heat. Stir constantly until boiling and then for a further 1 minute. Remove from heat and cover to stop skin forming on top.

Serving suggestion
Serve hot or cold with rhubarb or sliced bananas.

Variation
Poach peeled and quartered pears in a little pure orange juice. Pour hot custard into individual serving dishes and arrange pears on top. Serve chilled with a garnish of finely chopped mint mixed with grated orange rind, or a sliced strawberry with a few sultana grapes.

Rhubarb and Fruit Casserole

1 medium bunch rhubarb
2 oranges, peeled and sliced
into rounds
1 cup chopped dates
2 red apples, peeled and
sliced
1 cup orange juice

Trim, wash and chop rhubarb into chunks. Place into a large ovenproof dish in alternate layers with orange, dates and apples. Pour orange juice over. Cover and bake 190°C (375°F) about 30 minutes.

Serving suggestion
Serve hot or cold with Dessert Cream (page 58) or Vanilla Ice Cream (page 61).

N.B. Place foil under dish to catch any spillage.

Serves 6

Gramma Pudding

2 cups cooked cold gramma
   (about 1.5 kg uncooked)
rind of 1 lemon, finely
   grated
rind of 1 orange, finely
   grated
½ cup sultanas
¼ teaspoon cinnamon
¼ teaspoon nutmeg
¼ teaspoon ginger powder
½ cup orange juice
1 heaped tablespoon
   cornflour
4 egg whites, whipped

Place all ingredients, except egg whites, in a basin. Mix well, then fold through the egg whites. Place in a shallow ovenproof dish and bake at 200°C (400°F) about 30 minutes, depending on size and shape of dish. When cooked, the pudding will be firm to a light touch and nicely browned on top.

Serving suggestion
Serve hot or cold with Dessert Cream (page 58).

N.B. Gramma is a soft, watery variety of pumpkin generally used for desserts.

Serves 4

Zesty Bananas

4 bananas
1 large orange
finely chopped mint

Peel bananas and pierce all over. Place on foil. Finely grate rind of orange. Squeeze orange juice over bananas then sprinkle with rind. Seal foil and bake at 200°C (400°F) for 15 minutes.
   This recipe may be cooked on the barbecue.

Serving suggestion
Sprinkle lightly with mint and accompany with Dessert Cream (page 58).

Variations
Substitute apples, pears or peaches for the bananas. Remove pips, core or stone as applicable. Peel and quarter the fruit and proceed as above.

Serves 4

Rice Peaches and Cream

1½ cups cooked rice
2 cups skim milk
½ teaspoon vanilla essence
½ cup sultanas
1 can (420 g) peaches, with
  or without natural juice
Dessert Cream (page 58)
nutmeg
tiny sprigs of mint, for
  decoration

Save 4 peach slices, or pieces, for decoration. Over a medium heat, cook rice, milk, vanilla and sultanas until most of milk is absorbed. Roughly chop peaches and, including any natural juice, fold through. Extra juice will be absorbed.

Serving suggestion
Serve hot with Dessert Cream, or cool slightly and pour into parfait glasses alternately with Dessert Cream. Top with Dessert Cream, dust with nutmeg, decorate with peach slice, and mint sprig. Chill and serve.

Variation
Use any canned fruit* or fresh fruit.

* See cooking notes

Serves 4

Summertime Fruit Salad

1 cup seasonal fruits, cut
  into chunks

Place seasonal fruits into scooped out half of pineapple, pawpaw or rockmelon, or into glasses. Top with Ice Cream (page 61), low-fat natural yoghurt, or Dessert Cream (page 58).

Per person

Summer Fruit Tray

½ watermelon
1 pawpaw
1 rockmelon or canteloupe
2 red apples
2 large bananas
1 punnet strawberries
2 kiwi fruit
250 g muscatel grapes
1 orange, for juice

Select a large, attractive tray — preferably oval in shape. Make a centre line of watermelon, cut into triangles and overlapping. On either side, place slices of pawpaw and rockmelon or canteloupe, working towards the outside. At the moment of serving add to the tray unpeeled wedges of apple and thick slices of banana, both sprinkled with orange juice. Garnish with whole strawberries, kiwi fruit and frozen grapes.

To freeze grapes
Place small bunches of grapes, uncovered, in freezer for 24 hours. Remove from freezer only when serving. Grapes will 'blush' and should be eaten immediately.

Serves 4-6

Orange Rice Cream

1 cup cooked Cold Orange
  Rice (page 43)
1 cup Orange Dessert
  Cream (page 58)
1 ripe pear, peeled, cored
  and halved
1 cup sweet, seedless green
  grapes
1 orange (juice and finely
  grated rind)

Combine rice and Dessert Cream together. Place half the mixture in each of two sweet dishes. Place pear half on top and fill cavity with grapes. Squeeze juice from orange over and sprinkle rind on top to garnish.

Variations
Pear may be poached in a little orange juice to soften. Bananas cut into thin rounds may be substituted when grapes are out of season.
A little extra Dessert Cream may be served separately if desired.

Serves 2

CAKES AND SLICES

Apple and Cinnamon Scones

---

3 cups wholemeal self-
    raising flour
2 heaped teaspoons
    cinnamon
175 g cottage cheese
1 cup raisins
2 cups cooked apples (cold)
1 cup skim milk

Place flour and cinnamon in bowl. Crumble cheese into mixture, using fingertips and lifting high out of bowl. Add raisins, coating with flour mixture. Spread apple evenly over top. Add milk all at once and use a knife to mix quicky. Then use fingers to complete mixing. Place dough on floured board and knead lightly. Shape into oblong, place on floured tray and cut into 16 pieces. Brush tops with milk and bake in hot oven 225°C (450°F) for 20-25 minutes.

Serving Suggestion
Serve with Banana Dessert Cream (page 58).

Makes 16

Date Cupcakes

1½ cups chopped dates
1 cup orange juice
1 teaspoon vanilla essence
1 teaspoon lemon rind
1½ cups wholemeal self-
    raising flour
½ teaspoon cinnamon
½ teaspoon nutmeg
3 egg whites, whipped

Place dates and orange juice in saucepan and bring to boil. Lower heat and stir for 2-3 minutes. Allow to cool. Add remainder of ingredients in order, then fold in with a wooden spoon. Pile mixture into cupcake pans, making 12 large cakes. Bake at 210°C (425°F) for about 15 minutes.

Carrot and Orange Cake

200 g ricotta cheese*
3 egg whites
2 cups sultanas
1 large carrot, coarsely
    grated
1 medium orange, rind
    finely grated
2 tablespoons orange juice
1 teaspoon mixed spice
2 cups wholemeal self-
    raising flour
1 cup skim milk

Cream ricotta with egg whites in a food processor or electric mixer. Add all other ingredients and mix. Pour mixture into non-stick Swiss roll tin. Bake at 200°C (400°F) about 40 minutes, varying the time if a different shaped cake tin is used.

* See cooking notes

Carrot and Orange Slice

2 cups wholemeal self-
    raising flour
1 cup rolled oats
½ teaspoon mixed spice
1 cup raisins
1 cup sultanas
rind of one orange, grated
2 medium carrots, grated
    roughly
1 cup skim milk
2 tablespoons orange juice
½ teaspoon vanilla
2 egg whites

Place all dry ingredients in bowl. Place milk, orange juice, vanilla and egg whites in blender. Process for a few seconds. Pour over dry ingredients and mix well. Bake in non-stick Swiss roll tin at 175°C (325°F) for 40 minutes.

Orange Pumpkin Fruit Slice (page 69)
Date Scones (page 72)
Carob Sultana Cake (page 70)
Lemon Grass Tea (page 84)

Orange Pumpkin Fruit Slice

1½ **cups raisins**
1½ **cups sultanas**
1 **cup water**
1 **dessertspoon orange rind**
1 **cup cooked cold pumpkin,
    mashed**
2½ **cups wholemeal self-
    raising flour**
½ **cup cornflour**
1 **heaped teaspoon mixed
    spice**
3 **egg whites, whipped**
½ **cup skim milk**

Place fruit and water in large saucepan and simmer 2 or 3 minutes to plump fruit. Allow to cool (not cold). Add orange rind and pumpkin, folding them lightly into fruit. Combine flours and spice and add to mixture. Combine egg whites and milk, add to mixture and, using a wooden spoon, fold all through to mix. Bake in a non-stick slice tin in a moderate oven 190°C (375°F) for about 35 minutes.

Variation
May be cooked in a deeper cake tin allowing an extra 15 minutes, or until cooked.

N.B. Pumpkin must be very bright in colour and quite dry when mashed. New pumpkin is unsuitable.

Fruit Salad Cake

200 g **ricotta cheese***
3 **egg whites**
1 **cup Fruit Medley†**
1 **cup sultanas**
2 **cups wholemeal flour**
1 **cup orange juice**

Place ricotta cheese and egg whites in a food processor or mixer bowl, and process until well blended. Then add fruit, flour and juice and process until mixed well. Place in a non-stick cake pan and cook at 190°C (350°F) for 40 minutes.

† Health food shops and supermarkets sell a package of chopped dried apricots, pears and apples with a few sultanas which they call 'Fruit Medley'. This gives the cake a lovely fresh tangy flavour. If preferred, you may replace 'Medley' with other dried fruit, and orange juice with skim milk for a light fruit cake.

* See cooking notes.

Strawberry Smoothie, Carrot and Apple Juice, Orange Juice and Soda (pages 85/86)

After Dinner Carob Balls

4 tablespoons skim milk
  powder
3 tablespoons carob powder
2 tablespoons unprocessed
  bran
4 tablespoons sultanas
about 6 tablespoons cold
  water
prunes

Mix milk powder, carob and bran well, ensuring no lumps in carob. Add sultanas and mix. Then add water and mix. Open prunes, remove seeds and fill with mixture. Eat same day.

Variation
Roll balls in crushed Nabisco *Weeties*.

N.B. A little more or less water may be necessary to retain shape when making stuffing mix. A soft mixture is preferable.

Carob Sultana Cake

200 g ricotta cheese*
3 egg whites
3 heaped tablespoons carob
  powder
2 apples, grated
2 cups sultanas
1¾ cups wholemeal self-
  raising flour
¼ cup cornflour
1 cup skim milk
1 teaspoon vanilla essence

In a food processor or electric mixer, cream ricotta with egg whites, then add carob powder. Mix thoroughly. Reserving one grated apple, add all other ingredients to cheese mixture. Pour mixture into non-stick cake tin and top with grated apple. Bake at 200°C (400°F) for about 45 minutes, depending on size of tin.

* See cooking notes.

Carob Ricecake Nibbles

1 cup unsweetened carob
  buttons
1 teaspoon peppermint
  essence
4 rice cakes, broken into
  quarters*

Place carob buttons in heatproof dish and melt over water boiling in saucepan on cooktop. Add essence and stir. Then, using a knife, spread quickly over ricecake pieces. Store in an airtight jar for up to 3 days.

* Rice cakes are pure brown rice made into crisp, flat round cakes (available in health food shops and some supermarkets).

Afternoon Tea Cakes

100 g ricotta cheese*
4 unbeaten egg whites
½ cup chopped dates
1½ cups wholemeal self-
  raising flour

Place ricotta and egg whites in food processor and process until creamed. Add other ingredients all at once and mix. Spoon generously into non-stick cupcake pans, making 12 large cakes. Bake at 210°C (425°F) for about 20 minutes.

* See cooking notes.

Muesli Slice

4 cups muesli (page 1)
1 teaspoon mixed spice
2 tablespoons skim milk
  powder
2 tablespoons wholemeal
  self-raising flour
1 cup orange juice

Place dry ingredients in bowl and mix well. Add orange juice and mix again. Press mixture into non-stick Swiss-roll tin and bake at 175°C (350°F) for 25 minutes. Remove from oven, mark into slices while hot, and allow to cool. Then turn out on to cooling rack.

71

Date Scones

2 cups wholemeal self-
  raising flour
100 g ricotta cheese★
1½ cups chopped dates
1 cup skim milk

Place flour in large bowl. Lifting high, to allow air into mixture, and using tips of fingers, rub cheese into flour until it resembles breadcrumbs. Add dates, coating well with flour mixture. Add milk all at once, using a knife then tips of fingers to mix. Knead lightly on a floured board. Shape into an oblong about 2½ cm (1 inch) thick. Place on a floured tray and cut into 12. Bake high in a hot oven 225°C (450°F) about 20 minutes until golden.

Variation
Dried fruit salad medley (available at supermarkets and health food stores) may replace dates.

Serving suggestion
With a *little* pure jam★ or Apricot Spread (page 83) and Dessert Cream (page 58).

N.B. A good scone requires a very light touch and quick mixing. Scones must be mixed by hand. Do not use electric appliances.

★ See cooking notes.

Makes 12

BREADS, PASTRIES AND SANDWICHES

Sandwich Fillings

Pritikin* bread or rolls, or any other acceptable breads

This is a good way to finish leftovers. When making sandwiches, be very generous with fillings. No butter or margarine is to be used. Low-fat cottage cheese or ricotta is acceptable or, if eating immediately, Sour Cream Dressing (page 80) may be used. Each sandwich starts and finishes with thick layers of lettuce and beansprouts.

- Thick tomato slices with chopped fresh mint, chives, coriander, basil, oregano, or any other herbs.
- Apple (with a sprinkling of orange juice), raisins, celery, and grated carrot.
- Salmon or chicken, tomato, cucumber and onion rings.
- Coleslaw with chicken or fish and Sour Cream Dressing (page 80).
- Grated raw carrot, zucchini, beetroot, etc. previously sprinkled with herb vinegar.
- Leftover cold vegetables or patties, sliced capsicum and onion rings.
- Any combination of salad vegetables, with or without fresh herbs. If using dried herbs, use only a pinch.

Herb and Breadcrumb Seasoning

2 cups soft wholemeal
  breadcrumbs
1 medium onion, chopped
2 teaspoons mixed herbs
¼ cup chopped fresh
  parsley
1 egg white

Mix all ingredients together and use for filling the following:
- cabbage rolls
- capsicum
- fish
- crepes
- tomatoes
- zucchini
- poultry

Variations
Replace mixed herbs with 2 tablespoons chopped fresh herbs, singularly or in combinations:
- basil
- chives
- coriander
- lemon grass
- oregano
- mint
- rosemary
- lemon thyme

N.B. If necessary, when mixing, add a little water to seasoning.

Crustry Wholemeal Damper

2 cups wholemeal self-
  raising flour
1 cup skim milk
2 teaspoons dried onion
  flakes
1 teaspoon mixed herbs

Place flour in bowl with onion flakes and herbs. Lightly mix. Pour milk in, all at once. Mix quickly with a knife and then roll around with fingers to form a ball. Knead once or twice on a floured board. Form into a round, scone shape. Brush top with a little extra milk. Bake on a floured tray in a hot oven 230°C (475°F) for 20 minutes.

Serving suggestion
Serve warm with soup.

Variation
For a sweet damper, replace herbs with 1 teaspoon mixed spice and 1 cup sultanas.

Hot Vegi Luncheon Scone

1 cup wholemeal self-raising flour
1 medium onion, chopped and lightly cooked
1 cup chopped chives
½ cup liquid skim milk
3 egg whites, whipped
1 medium carrot, grated
1 medium zucchini, grated
1 medium tomato, thinly sliced

In a bowl, place flour, onions, and ½ cup of chives. Fold in slightly. Add milk and egg whites together and mix. Pour mixture into non-stick shallow 20 cm (8 inch) pie dish. Sprinkle with grated vegetables. Arrange tomato slices on top, then sprinkle on remaining chives. Bake in a hot oven 220°C (425°F) about 20 minutes, or until cooked. Serve immediately.

Serving suggestion
Serve hot with steamed vegetables or salad, or cold with salad.

Variation
Use other fresh herbs or vegetables to taste.

Serves 4

Susan's Savoury Toasties

To make toasties, cut bread into small shapes. Place on tray in the oven and bake at 120°C (250°F) for about ½ hour, or until lightly browned. Top with the following:
• Cold, cooked green peas in Sour Cream Dressing (page 80), flavoured with chopped mint *or* garlic.
• Spread toasties with ricotta cheese. Sprinkle with chopped chives. Cut tiny petal shapes from capsicum and arrange flower-fashion on top.
• Mix finely-chopped apple and celery with ricotta cheese. Top with a little grated carrot.
• Mix lots of finely-chopped shallots with ricotta cheese. Top with a little Geska cheese.
• Spread toasties with ricotta cheese. Top with pineapple pieces and chopped mint.

N.B. See cooking notes about ricotta cheese.

Toasted Asparagus Roll Ups

9 slices Pritikin* bread
   (crusts removed)
9 asparagus spears, steamed
   (or canned, unsalted)
Geska cheese

Bread should be *very* fresh so it will fold over without breaking. Place 1 asparagus spear in each piece of bread, sprinkle with geska, and fold bread over, fastening with a toothpick. Place on tray in moderate oven 200°C (400°F) and bake about 15-20 minutes until golden and crisp. Remove toothpicks and serve.

Serving suggestion
Serve as an entree with a little lemon White Sauce (page 79) spooned over and accompanied by a green salad, or as a main meal with Garlic Spinach and Rice (page 33) and steamed new potatoes.

Variation
Any leftovers may be used as fillings, e.g. mixed vegetables with a sprinkling of mixed herbs, or Tuna and Savoury Toast (page 56).

N.B. Bread may be warmed in microwave to allow easier handling.

Serves 3

Garlic Toast

2 slices wholemeal toast
ricotta cheese*
dried garlic flakes

Spread hot toast with ricotta and sprinkle with garlic flakes. Place under griller for 1 minute only. Serve immediately.

Variation: Savoury Toast
As above, including a sprinkling of dried oregano leaves. Grilling takes only 30 seconds, as this combination burns quicky. Watch constantly. Serve immediately.

Instant Garlic Toast

Take hot wholemeal toast and quicky rub liberally on
both sides with fresh peeled whole garlic cloves. Serve
immediately.

Three Flours Pastry Case

Select
500 g wheat grains
350 g rye grains
250 g buckwheat grains
  (raw)

Base and sides
1½ cups flour with enough
  liquid to just moisten, for
  thin layer

Topping
¾ cup flour with enough
  liquid for thick pouring
  consistency

Find a healthfood store with a grinding machine.
  Ask for the grains to be mixed and fineground into
flour★. Combine flour with water or fruit juice to
make desired consistency.

Quantity for 20 cm (8 inch) shallow pie dish
Place base mixture in dish and, with the back of a
spoon, spread and press thinly into shape of dish.
Place in moderate oven 175°C (375°F) for 10 minutes.
Remove from oven and place hot filling into case.
Spoon topping over and spread thinly to meet sides.
Replace in oven and cook 10 minutes.

Serving suggestion
Apple Pie (page 57).

★ Store flour in refrigerator.

Hot Herb Rolls

1 Pritikin* bread roll
ricotta cheese*
mixed herbs

Cut roll vertically into 3 pieces. Spread each piece with ricotta cheese and sprinkle with mixed herbs. Place pieces together to re-form roll. Wrap in foil and bake about 10 minutes—long enough to heat through. Serve immediately.

N.B. Fresh or dried herbs may be used.

Variation
Mix herbs with non-fat natural yoghurt. Cut into roll without going all the way through. Part the slices and fill the cavities with the yoghurt mixture. Brush the top with a little extra mixture and bake unwrapped until crisp, about 10-15 minutes. Serve immediately. If desired, fresh chopped garlic could be substituted for herbs.

* See cooking notes.

Per person

Chicken Open Hawaiian on Pritikin*

1 slice Pritikin* bread
lettuce leaves
1 slice unsweetened
**   pineapple**
½ cup cooked chicken
¼ cup chopped celery
¼ cup grated carrot
¼ teaspoon ginger powder
Sour Cream Dressing
**   (page 80)**
1 medium red apple,
**   unpeeled and sliced**

Place lettuce, and then pineapple, on bread. Mix chicken, celery, carrot, and ginger powder with a little Sour Cream Dressing to bind and place on top. Garnish with apple slices and serve immediately.

Variation
Rice or fish may replace chicken.
Potato Salad (page 11) may be served as an extra.

Per person

SAUCES AND ACCOMPANIMENTS

Basic White Sauce

---

2 cups skim milk
1 rounded tablespoon
cornflour

Mix ¼ cup milk with cornflour until smooth. Set aside. Place remainder of milk in saucepan and heat until almost boiling. Remove from heat and add cornflour mixture, stirring quicky to avoid lumps. Place saucepan over heat and keep stirring until sauce boils. Then reduce heat and cook 1 minute longer. If lumps occur, smooth by beating for one minute with an eggbeater.

Variations
Suggested ingredients to add to sauce:
1 cup button mushrooms, sliced.
½ cup chopped parsley with juice of 1 lemon.
1 small onion, chopped, with juice of 1 lemon.
½ cup chopped fresh chives.

Serving suggestions
Spoon over fish, chicken or steamed vegetables.
Add chopped, cooked fish or chicken to sauce and fill Crepes (page 58) or vegetables, e.g. capsicums, tomatoes or Jacket Baked Potatoes (page 29).

2 cups

Basic Sour Cream Dressing

½ cup non-fat natural
   yoghurt
½ cup cottage cheese

Thoroughly mix to a cream. Consistency is determined by adding more yoghurt to make cream firm or less if you wish to pour it.

Variations
Add the following to the basic dressing and mix thoroughly. Allow to stand at least 1 hour.

Island Pink *(with salad)*

¼ cup tomato puree
2 tablespoons lemon juice
2 drops tabasco sauce
1 tablespoon finely chopped onion
1 tablespoon finely chopped green
   capsicum

Green Mayo *(with salad)*

½ cup finely chopped fresh herbs.
Some good combinations are:
Basil with oregano and garlic.
Lemon grass with a pinch of chilli powder.
Mint with a few pieces of finely chopped
   unsweetened pineapple.
½ cup each of chives and shallots.

Horseradish Cream
(with cabbage rolls)

1 tablespoon pure horseradish
1 tablespoon chopped parsley
1 tablespoon grated carrot

Cucumber and Garlic
(with hot, steamed vegetables)

½ cup finely chopped cucumber
crushed or finely chopped garlic to
   taste (as much as you like)

Tomato Capsicum Relish

3 medium tomatoes,
   roughly chopped
½ green capsicum, chopped
½ cup chopped shallots
½ cup chopped coriander
   leaves
¼ teaspoon garam masala
1 tablespoon lemon juice

Mix all together. May be gently heated if desired.

Serving suggestion
Serve cold as a side dish for curry or salad, or hot as an extra side vegetable for poached fish (pages 52/53).

Sour Cream and Garlic Dressing

2 large cloves of garlic
1 cup of Sour Cream
   Dressing (page 80)

Peel and finely chop garlic. Then stir into Sour Cream Dressing.

Variation
Replace garlic with chopped fresh herbs, e.g. mint, chives, basil.

Lemon and Garlic Dressing

2 large cloves of garlic
½ cup lemon juice

Peel and finely chop garlic. Then stir into lemon juice.

Serving suggestions
Pour over steamed hot or cold beetroot, or use as a salad dressing.

Mint Sauce

boiling water (a small
   amount)
½ cup fresh chopped mint
½ cup apple cider vinegar

Pour boiling water over mint so it is just covered. Cool slightly, then add vinegar.

N.B. Boiling water brings out the mint flavour.

Serving suggestion
Use with steamed peas or spinach.

Makes 1 cup.

Yoghurt Toast Toppings

low-fat skim milk yoghurt
wholemeal bread slices
choice of:
chopped fresh chives
chopped garlic cloves
Geska cheese
Geska cheese with dried
   onion flakes

Use as a topping for vegetable dishes or as a nibble.

Topping pieces
To the yoghurt, add any of the suggested toppings and fold through. Brush over bread to coat liberally on both sides. Cut bread into small pieces about 1.5 cm (½ inch). Fifteen minutes before completion of oven-cooked meal, pile topping pieces evenly over, and replace in oven to cook until crisp.

Serving suggestion
Crunchy Vegetarian Pie (page 33).
Pepita, Bean and Vegetable Delight (page 36).

Topping crumbs
Brush soft breadcrumbs with the mixture and bake on a non-stick tray in a moderate oven 200°C (400°F), for about 5 minutes, until crisp.

Serving suggestion
Sprinkle hot over steamed vegetables or cold over salad, or use as a coating for Salmon Rissoles (page 54).

Nibble
After coating the bread with the mixture, cut into shapes and bake on a non-stick tray, in a moderate oven 200°C (400°F) for about 15-20 minutes, until crisp. Flip them over once during cooking. Cool and store in airtight jar.

Serving suggestion
Serve with drinks.

N.B. Be generous with herbs or cheese. Use equal quantities of fresh herbs with yoghurt, i.e. ½ cup yoghurt, ½ cup chopped herbs.
    Use a liberal sprinkling of Geska cheese, i.e. ½ cup yoghurt, 1 teaspoon cheese, 1 teaspoon dried onion flakes.
    The above quantities will coat about 4 slices of bread.

Apricot Spread

Any quantity of dried apricots, covered with water

Cover and simmer, stirring occasionally to avoid catching. Simmer until water has been absorbed and apricots can be mashed into a spread.*

Serving suggestion
Use as a spread for toast, scones, etc. or added to chicken recipe (page 42).

Variation
Any dried fruits may be substituted. If sweetening is desired, a few finely chopped dates could be added.

N.B. Spread sparingly to keep triglycerides low.

* Store in refrigerator.

Basic Tomato Sauce

2 cans (each 410 g) tomatoes (chopped)
2 heaped tablespoons Tomato Magic*
1 large, or 6 small, cloves garlic
1 medium onion, chopped
1 medium green capsicum, chopped
1 rounded teaspoon dried basil leaves
1 rounded teaspoon dried oregano leaves
3 large bay leaves
¼ cup finely chopped fresh parsley

Place all ingredients except parsley in saucepan. Cover and bring to the boil on moderate heat. Reduce heat and simmer 30 minutes or longer, up to 60 minutes if time allows. Remove bay leaves and serve with parsley sprinkled over sauce.

Serving suggestions
An accompaniment to pasta dishes such as lasagna, cannelloni and spaghetti.
Spoon over steamed, mixed vegetables.

* See cooking notes.

6 cups

DRINKS

Tea, Coffee or Hot Chocolate Substitute

With freshly boiled water, hot skim milk or both, use one teaspoon per cup of the following (or other 'legal' substitutes):

Dried Linden Tea
Nature's Cuppa★
Ecco★
Carob powder
Rooitea★ (pronounced Roy-Tee)

N.B. Caffeine products are not used. Even decaffeinated products may be suspect because of processing used to remove the caffeine. Recommended are Dried Linden Tea (used at the Pritikin★ Clinic), coffee substitutes and dried or fresh herbal teas.

Herbal Tea

Some suggested ingredients:
1 piece of lemon rind (not grated) approximately the size of a bay leaf
1 bay leaf
sprig of mint
lemon grass
basil
rosemary

Place fresh herbs to taste in cup or teapot. Pour boiling water over and allow to steep. (The first three ingredients may be used separately or in combination.)

84

Juices

Juices should not replace your daily fruit and vegetable intake. They are intended as 'between meals' drinks and should be drunk within 15 minutes of being made. Fruit juices should be diluted about half-and-half with water, soda water or mineral water because of their high natural sugar content.

You should start drinking vegetable juices gradually, drinking them diluted with water or in small concentrated amounts to let your body get used to them.

For more information on juicing and suggested combinations, I recommend Dr N. Walker's book, *Fresh Fruit and Vegetable Juices*.

A 'dedicated' juicer is essential; blenders, etc are not suitable. As with the food processor, the more powerful the motor, the better.

Some suggested vegetable combinations

- Carrot
- Carrot and apple
- Carrot, celery and endive
- Carrot spinach and beetroot

Vegetables should be scrubbed clean; beetroot may be peeled to eliminate the earthy taste. Large, old carrots are recommended because of their higher vitamin A content.

Thirst Quenchers

Place some ice in a chilled glass. Half-fill with unsweetened or fresh fruit juice. Fill to top with water, soda water or mineral water. Garnish with a slice of apple, orange, pineapple or mint.

Smoothies

Pour a large glass of cold skim milk into a blender adding ice cubes and/or Vanilla Ice Cream (page 61).
   Add any of the following:

- 1 ripe banana
- 1 cup strawberries
- 2 ripe peaches
- 4 ripe apricots

Process until thoroughly whipped.

Variation
1 tablespoon of carob powder. Add skim milk ice cubes when serving.

Party Punch

1 can (850 mL) unsweetened
   fruit cocktail
1 can (850 mL) unsweetened
   pineapple juice
2 cups chopped fresh fruit
8 tiny sprigs mint
ice cubes
2 bottles chilled soda water

Place first five ingredients in a large bowl. Add soda water immediately prior to serving (so that the punch does not go flat).

Variation
Use flavoured ice cubes made with pure or diluted unsweetened fruit juices or, if available, pure or diluted passionfruit pulp. When frozen, turn cubes out, place into freezer bags and store in the freezer. Slight shrinkage may occur but the flavour is retained.

INDEX